pg 137

UNSPORTSMANLIKE CONDUCT

UNSPORTSMANLIKE CONDUCT

The National Collegiate Athletic Association and the Business of College Football

PAUL R. LAWRENCE

PRAEGER

New York
Westport, Connecticut
London

Library of Congress Cataloging-in-Publication Data

Lawrence, Paul R.
  Unsportsmanlike conduct.

  Bibliography: p.
  Includes index.
  1. National Collegiate Athletic Association.
  2. College sports—Economic aspects—United States.
  3. College sports—Moral and ethical aspects—United
States. I. Title.
  GV351.L38 1987   796.332'63'06073   87-12496
  ISBN 0-275-92725-3 (alk. paper)

Library of Congress Catalog Card Number: 87-12496
ISBN: 0-275-92725-3

First published in 1987

Praeger Publishers, One Madison Avenue, New York, NY 10010
A division of Greenwood Press, Inc.

Printed in the United States of America

The paper used in this book complies with the Permanent Paper Standard issued by the National Information Standards Organization
(Z39.48-1984).

10 9 8 7 6 5 4 3 2 1

Contents

List of Tables

Acknowledgments

I am grateful to many people — too many to mention by name — who helped and encouraged me with this book. Prominent among this group are my parents and wife, Ann, who joined me while this work was in progress. I also am indebted to Robert D. Tollison, who ignited my interest in the economics of college sports; Dwight Lee, who ensured I completed my doctoral dissertation, which was the basis for this book; Ruth B. Haas and John Swinton, who helped shaped this book; and John L. Lanphear, who produced the tables.

Introduction

The National Collegiate Athletic Association (NCAA) is the single most powerful force in intercollegiate sports in the United States. Its rules and tournaments are synonymous with amateur athletics. It either directly regulates or strongly influences all aspects of college athletics in this country. It dictates the number of games a team can play, it specifies what a university may give a recruited athlete, it restricts the number of athletic grants-in-aid a university may offer and limits the amount of these athletic awards. Until 1984, it also governed the televising of college football games. The Association maintains a Department of Enforcement that investigates reports of rule violations and penalizes the violators. These penalties may range in severity from a private reprimand to exclusion from championship tournaments to banishment from the Association.

Despite its pervasive role in college athletics, there has been, to date, no comprehensive study of how the NCAA came to fill this role or, more important, what its policies have meant for those most directly affected by them—the students who are also athletes.

These athletes were originally the reason the NCAA was formed. By the turn of the last century, football had become the most violent intercollegiate sport in the country. Players wore no protective equipment, and because their tactics included striking, gouging, and butting one another, serious injuries were common. The 1905 football season concluded with enough fatal and near fatal injuries to galvanize an increasingly uneasy public. Told by President Theodore Roosevelt either to reform the sport or abandon it, representatives of 13 colleges and universities met in New York City that December to decide the fate of the game. They agreed that under the proper conditions intercollegiate athletic competition could benefit everyone involved, and they formed the Intercollegiate Athletic Association of the United States (IAAUS), which became the NCAA in 1910, to specifically remove violence from football.

At first, the NCAA limited its activities to standardizing the rules of the various sports. But gradually the Association's responsibilities expanded until it reached its current dominant position in college athletics. In order to document the development and structure of this industry, I decided to conduct a study of college athletics. Because of the power of the NCAA, I found my attempt to explain the organization of this industry becoming an effort to explain the emergence and the behavior of the NCAA in relation to college football. I began to weigh two economic theories that could be used to interpret the Association's behavior.

THEORY 1: THE INTERNALIZATION OF AN INTRAINDUSTRY EXTERNALITY

First, I believe that the NCAA was organized to internalize an intra-industry externality (that is, solve an industrywide problem)—the injuries resulting from football teams playing according to different rules. This argument for industrywide action holds that when two or more competing ideas or systems exist, society forgoes the benefits from the use of only one idea or system. Reacting to this tendency, members of an industry meet to decide which idea or system to adopt so as to act more efficiently.

The U.S. version of football evolved through refinements in the English sport of rugby, and while early athletic associations tried to develop standard rules, the nonbinding nature of those rules and continuous experimenting with skills and techniques made it difficult to achieve any general agreement on standards of competitive conduct. As a result, teams had to learn one or more sets of rules. This troublesome task kept many colleges from competing and reduced the number of games. Furthermore, the lack of standard rules invited the dangerous playing tactics, which were partly to blame for the deaths and serious injuries that occurred in the late 1800s and early 1900s.

By agreeing to standardize the rules, the schools (football producers) internalized an externality (injuries). Consistent with economic theory, they did so because all of them (the industry's producers) were affected and all of them expected standardized rules to produce a game that more people would want to watch (that is, the demand for the contests would increase). Thus, we can interpret the establishment of the association soon to be known as the NCAA as an attempt to internalize an intraindustry externality.

Were its objectives merely to address intraindustry externalities, however, the Association would never have involved itself in such elements as payments to student-athletes, the length of the seasonal schedule, or television broadcasts of college football contests. But whatever the accuracy of the idea that the NCAA first met to internalize an intraindustry externality—and we shall see shortly that its early actions remained consistent with this theory—the Association gradually focused on matters that did not constitute externalities generated by college sports. As it developed an intricate network of regulations governing intercollegiate sports in the United States, and as it organized an agency to investigate member institutions and punish those who violated its rules, the NCAA's behavior departed from that of an association that seeks only to address problems common to the industry.

THEORY 2: THE NCAA AS A BUSINESS CARTEL

My second theory presents the NCAA as an intercollegiate athletic cartel, an interpretation I base on the well-established economic principle that characterizes as a cartel producers colluding to restrict output in an effort to raise prices and profits. This theory also presupposes that a cartel needs a mechanism to enforce restrictive agreements because once a cartel forms, there are financial incentives for each participant to violate its agreements.

In competitive markets, firms compete by trying to sell the best product at the lowest price in order to capture a large market share and earn substantial profits. As more firms compete this way, they increase their operating costs and decrease the price of their product (the firms collectively increase the amount of the product available, thus forcing down its price). This competition forces profits to shrink.

Against this threat, the firms may decide to organize a cartel. By restricting competition, they can sell a more expensive product produced with lower material and salary costs. In short, businesses that operate in a cartelized market enjoy larger profits because they limit competition.

Cartel theory holds that collective behavior evolves when producers of the same product meet to promote efficiency and save costs. Seen in the light of cartel theory, the early years of the NCAA can be interpreted as the time when the producers first organized to promote their own continuing collective action. Characterized by intercollege meetings and correspondence, these early NCAA years constituted the requisite behavior of competitors comparing notes before establishing a market-sharing agreement.

Cartel theory also provides an explanation for the restrictions on wages paid to student-athletes, the length of the regular and postseason schedules, and the later decisions regarding television coverage. Classic cartel theory describes methods such as these as restricting competition and transferring income from consumers (the fans) or employees (the student-athletes) to producers (the athletic departments). In addition, cartel theory explains, far better than any other idea, the many regulations the NCAA adopted after World War II, the time when the NCAA clearly recognized the economic benefits the producers received as the rules governing conduct increased in number and intricacy.

Of the possible explanations, only cartel theory explains the development of the enforcement mechanism the NCAA uses to investigate and punish rule violators. A school has an obvious incentive to cheat on any NCAA agreement: a competitive advantage over those schools that follow the agreement. Hence, in accordance with cartel theory, once the NCAA adopted a detailed set of rules prescribing how a school must behave, it had to establish an enforcement mechanism to ensure that all its members followed those rules.

The standard historical studies of college athletics since the 1880s tend to highlight athletes and their dramatic performances at the expense of the fascinating network of rules and regulations that produced these performances and controlled their exposure through television. Nevertheless, viewed economically, the history of the NCAA compels the conclusion that cartel theory offers the best explanation for its organization and for the existence of the modern college athletics industry.

AN EMERGING CONSENSUS

As I conducted this examination I found that other economists had also discovered that the NCAA behaved like a cartel. Armen Alchian and William Allen, for example, point out that the agreement among universities that restricts the wages of student-athletes is characteristic of a cartel.[1] They claim that cartel conformity promotes a university's very existence.

Any college on probation or expelled would find it more expensive to recruit faculty, and students would be dissuaded from attending. Even Phi Beta Kappa refused to authorize chapters at colleges that gave disproportionate amounts of money to athletic scholarships. The survival of the college could be threatened.[2]

James V. Koch, however, took exception to Alchian and Allen's analysis: "There is little evidence," he said, "that NCAA sanctions and penalties have caused any state university to lose accreditation or financial support."[3] He prefers to analyze intercollegiate athletics by recognizing that it "approximates a cartel" and points out that the NCAA attempts to pool and divide cartel profits and inform all cartel members of market conditions and business and accounting techniques.[4]

Elsewhere, sociologist George H. Sage has focused on the restrictions on the wages paid to athletes under NCAA rules.[5] Drawing on Koch's analysis, Sage has observed that "College athletes ... cannot sell their skills on the open market ... because there is a wage limit all cartel members observe."[6] Sage concluded by noting that while official NCAA ideology touts its promotion of amateur sports, its operative goals involve the maximization of power and "oppression over student-athletes."[7]

While Koch, Sage, and others have made significant contributions in this area, their work has appeared in mostly academic journals and, therefore, has had a limited audience and scope.[8] Because of this, many important issues — concerning the growth of the NCAA, its success, its internal disputes, and its general avoidance of outside interference — have been omitted in these discussions and analyses. Here I examine these unaddressed topics and provide additional insights into issues previously discussed in the literature.

UNSPORTSMANLIKE CONDUCT

While doing my research, I was impressed by the tremendous changes that have taken place within college sports during the tenure of the NCAA. The NCAA has turned college sports into big business, with pressure to cheat on recruiting rules, to keep academically unfit students eligible, and to retain coaches who win but who sometimes do not exemplify the values generally believed to come from athletics.

At the turn of the century, college football players were students and the coaches were graduate students or teachers. Today, while a university's football coach often earns a salary in the hundreds of thousands of dollars, the NCAA seems most efficient when it is enacting rules to limit the compensation provided to the athletes who play the game. Coupled with an antitrust conviction for the organization of a collective television policy, it is clear that an organization once dominated by altruistically motivated people concerned only with the "good of the game" is now functioning like most other businesses, concentrating on product demand, competition, and employees' wages.

Given this record, it appears that the NCAA, which has been careful to avoid actions with punitive legal ramifications, is nevertheless guilty of violating the spirit under which it was formed. Unsportsmanlike conduct, however, is the football penalty for actions that violate the spirit of the rules, but not necessarily any specific rule. Hence, the title of this book.

NOTES

1. Armen Alchian and William Allen, *Exchange and Production: Competition, Coordination, and Control,* 2nd ed. (Belmont, Calif.: Wadsworth, 1969), 411.

2. Ibid.

3. James V. Koch, "The Economics of 'Big Time' Intercollegiate Athletics," *Social Science Quarterly* 52 (1971): 249.

4. Ibid. Koch's pioneering application of economics to college sports secured his position as a recognized authority in this area; because of this he was a key witness for the plaintiffs in the antitrust lawsuit filed by the Universities of Georgia and Oklahoma against the NCAA. *Board of Regents of Oklahoma and the University of Georgia Athletic Association v. NCAA,* 546 F. Supp. 1276 (1982).

5. George H. Sage, "The Intercollegiate Sports Cartel and Its Consequences," in *The Governance of Intercollegiate Athletics,* ed. James H. Frey (West Point, N.Y.: Leisure Press, 1982), 131-43.

6. Ibid., 135.

7. Ibid., 138.

8. James H. Frey's *The Governance of Intercollegiate Athletics,* (West Point, N.Y.: Leisure Press, 1982) contains a good collection of articles about the different aspects of intercollegiate sports.

UNSPORTSMANLIKE CONDUCT

CHAPTER 1

The Association's Formation and Its Early Years

FOOTBALL AND THE EARLY ATHLETIC ASSOCIATIONS

In stark contrast to the pomp and pageantry of modern inter-collegiate athletics, college athletics began rather inauspiciously. The first mention of athletic contests among U.S. college students appears in the records of a Princeton faculty meeting in May 1761, with the faculty members expressing annoyance with students who were "playing at ball." One finds no extensive discussion of competitive team sports, however, before 1820, at which time an "authoritative reference to football as a college pastime" was made.[1]

At first, cross-country running and gymnastics were the most popular college sports, with only intracollege competition taking place. But games of "football" are believed to have been played between college classes (for example, the freshmen versus the sophomores) at West Point, Harvard, Yale, Princeton, Amherst, and Bowdoin in the early and mid-1800s. This sport initially consisted of two teams, each with a large number of participants, who struggled for possession of an inflated animal bladder. These contests included few rules, and because most action by the participants involved kicking, they closely resembled soccer.[2]

The first intercollegiate athletic contest in any sport took place in 1852 when Harvard defeated Yale in a two-mile, eight-oared barge race on Lake Winnipesaukee, New Hampshire. The first intercollegiate football game was played on November 6, 1869, between Princeton and Rutgers at Rutgers's field in New Brunswick, New Jersey. Each team fielded 25 members, and the game required them to kick or butt the ball. Six goals constituted a victory, and, while descriptions of the teams indicate that Princeton was the physically superior team, Rutgers won the game six goals to four. In a rematch two weeks later, Princeton won with two goals to spare, eight to zero.[3]

In the 1870s football evolved out of the rules of both soccer and English rugby. The first set of intercollegiate football rules was compiled on October 19, 1873, by representatives of Harvard, Yale, Columbia, Princeton, and Rutgers. Experience derived from drawing up this initial set of rules later helped each school, except Rutgers, gain a position on the first football rules committee to be sanctioned by a football association.

During the 1870s football gained popularity as more schools began intercollegiate play. The nation's oldest and most traditional rivalry got under way when Harvard played Yale at New Haven, Connecticut, on November 13, 1875, before 2,000 paying spectators. Harvard defeated Yale four goals to none in a game that still closely resembled rugby.

Princeton adopted English rugby, devoid of incipient Americanisms, in mid-1876 as the official game of its "football club." Princeton then invited Harvard, Yale, and Columbia to send representatives to Springfield, Massachusetts, for a conference over a proposed football association. The association Princeton wished to organize would allow the colleges to standardize the rules of the game. All the invited schools sent representatives to the 1876 Springfield meeting, which produced the first forerunner of the National Collegiate Athletic Association (NCAA), the Intercollegiate Football Association (IFA).

The IFA adopted the basic rules of the Rugby Union, but the representatives added rules detailing how a winner would be determined, how many officials would be present, and how a contest would be timed.[4] Fierce debate took place over the number of players to a team. Yale suggested 11, while the rest of the IFA preferred the 15 players outlined in the Rugby Union Code. The issue was so important to Yale that it declined to join the IFA when it was outvoted. As a result, Columbia, Harvard, and Princeton became the original members of the IFA, and Yale did not join until 1879.

Nonetheless, the IFA provided a useful forum during the late 1800s for its members to meet and discuss the rules and techniques of the sport. During this time, college football changed rapidly as various adaptations in rugby skills produced many innovations in the American game. Much of the credit for the emergence of the U.S. sport of college football from English rugby belongs to the early members of the IFA:

To Harvard goes the credit for taking up Rugby and playing it consistently.... To Princeton belongs the credit of initiating the calling of the Convention.... And to Yale belongs the credit of persistently contending that the number of players on a team should be fixed at eleven.[5]

At least once a year from 1876 until its disbanding in 1894, the IFA met to change and update the rules of football. During this early period, intercollegiate athletics belonged exclusively to the students, and no faculty members attended the IFA meetings. Undergraduates were the first to manage their sport, but as the first generation of student managers graduated, graduate students and, inevitably, alumni remained to manage and direct the contests. Meanwhile, during the last quarter of the nineteenth century, faculty members kept resolutely aloof from athletic issues, and some sports historians speculate that this lack of faculty influence over college athletics partially explains the evils and abuses that marred the early period of intercollegiate football.[6]

Though Yale was not yet a member of the IFA, it continued to send a delegation led by Walter Camp to the early meetings. Camp, who would later be called the father of American football for his innovative ideas, lobbied unsuccessfully for four years for rule changes that would reduce the size of the teams and the field and alter the method of awarding points.[7] In 1880, Camp finally succeeded. At his recommendation, the IFA adopted rule changes that included decreasing both the size of the field and the number of players per team, and the adoption of 11-man teams brought Yale into the IFA that year. Another 1880 rule change allowed the ball to be put into play by directing it backward from its resting position. Thus the position in the middle of the line became the center, and a new position, quarterback, designated the person who handled the backward snap from the center.

In the late 1870s the number of schools playing football increased considerably, with newcomers to the game including Stevens, Tufts, City College of New York, Wesleyan, Pennsylvania, Trinity, Brown, Amherst, Pennsylvania Military College, Dartmouth, and Williams. The popularity of football quickly spread beyond the Northeast. The South's first game pitted Virginia Military Institute against Washington and Lee in 1877, while the first game in the Midwest took place in 1878 between Michigan and Racine.[8]

Through trial and error and with the desire of football officials to elevate a general interest in the game, the rules of football were continually revised. Among the major changes to reduce the game's inherent boredom were rules designed to prevent delays, the introduction of downs and yards to gain, the imposition of penalties for rule violations, and periodic reevaluations of the scoring system.

In 1884 the V-trick, or wedge, first appeared in a college football game, and historians credit both Princeton and Lehigh for its invention. The maneuver required seven players to lock arms and form a V with the ballcarrier shielded on the inside. The tip of the formation pointed downfield and moved forward, virtually unstoppable. The V-trick necessitated the first interference (that is to say, blocking) in football, a radical departure from the sport's habit of following English rugby, which prohibited blocking.

At the 1888 rules convention, Walter Camp sought to allow the defense to tackle the ballcarrier anywhere above the knees. Tackling below the waist had been prohibited, and with low tackling forbidden, teams could spread their offensive formations across the entire field. High tackling consequently brought speed to football and a playing style future generations would call wide open.

With the introduction of Camp's low tackling, however, offensive formations contracted, and the game grew more conservative. Now more susceptible to low tackles, large ballcarriers could no longer bowl over a high tackler, and the lateral passing that characterized rugby gradually disappeared as play became tighter. In addition, the widespread use of blocking contributed to the game's new style, even though rule changes prohibited blockers from extending their arms. Other rule changes enacted in 1888 sought to increase equipment safety and the number of officials.

Nevertheless, low tackling and the tightened player groupings made football a rougher, more dangerous game. But solutions to this problem divided the IFA members, and while they used temporary remedies, the issue had been only partially resolved when the introduction of the forward pass encouraged teams to use more of the playing field and to "open up" the game once again.

Also in 1888, Amos Alonzo Stagg enrolled in Yale's Divinity School and made the varsity football team as the starting right end. Stagg, a talented athlete, had never played football, but learned quickly and was voted all-American the next year. He never completed Yale Divinity but went on to earn fame as the football coach at the University of Chicago. His contributions to the game included inventing the tackling dummy and introducing the hidden ball trick. Interestingly, in 1891 he coached a team that had a center named James Naismith, who invented basketball the next year.[9]

In 1892, Lorin F. Deland, a Boston construction engineer who never actually played football but who had studied military strategy and was a chess expert, introduced football's most dangerous technique. If the V-trick or wedge worked well, he reasoned, it would work even better if the players forming the V got a 20-yard running start. The technique was first introduced in the 1892 Harvard-Yale game, and by 1893 most teams had adopted Deland's flying wedge, causing game injuries to increase dramatically. The attendant publicity was so harmful to the sport that the University Athletic Club of New York invited Harvard, Yale, Princeton, and Pennsylvania to form an altogether new rules committee.

The new committee subsequently made what A. A. Stagg called "the most sweeping rule revisions in ten years."[10] It outlawed the wedge, or V-trick, and the flying wedge and restricted mass momentum play. It reduced the length of a game from 90 to 70 minutes, and divided a contest into halves of 35 minutes. A linesman was also added to the referee and umpire as a third official.

These rule changes did not, however, halt the mass play causing all the injuries. Instead, the new rules only slowed these plays by preventing running starts. Mass play continued to cause injuries, which continued to prompt press and public outcries over the brutality of the sport. Mass play also caused problems for the IFA, which was still trying to establish a standardized set of football rules, because some members (like Harvard and Pennsylvania) sought to retain mass play while others (like Yale and Princeton) wanted to abolish it.

While it may seem odd that a school would retain a style of play that caused injuries, some explanation lies in the ability of a rival school to cope with that style of play. The football teams from Yale and Princeton had been troubled by opponents who used mass play; accordingly, Yale and Princeton had an interest both in eliminating this style of play and in writing rule changes that would make their teams more competitive.

Harvard and Pennsylvania, on the other hand, had pioneered techniques to deal with mass play, techniques that gave them a competitive advantage. The University of Pennsylvania used these techniques so efficiently that between 1894 and 1896 they lost only 1 of the 41 contests they played, allowing 68 points in this three-year span.[11]

Differences in each IFA member's approach to the rules of the game and the methods of determining player eligibility placed increasing pressure on the young association, but the first real strain centered on the use of graduate students. In 1889, Harvard and Princeton charged each other with using nonamateurs. An IFA investigation and certain rule changes caused both schools to drop their charges, but the incident caused bitter feelings among all involved, and Harvard withdrew from the association shortly thereafter.

The final straw for the IFA came in late 1893, when Pennsylvania withdrew in the dispute over mass play and eligibility rules proposed by Yale. Harvard and Pennsylvania invited Cornell to withdraw and form a rules committee. Only Yale and Princeton, both of whom had little influence in intercollegiate athletics at the time, remained in the Association, and the IFA officially disbanded in 1894.

With the disbanding of the IFA, many new rules committees appeared, and while various groups of eastern schools sought to assert control over football, for the first time other sections of the country — notably California and the Midwest — established their own governing bodies. The most productive of these efforts came from the Western Intercollegiate Athletic Conference, the forerunner of the Big Ten, formed in 1895. The conference schools established rules governing freshman eligibility and the number of years an athlete could participate in a sport. They also eliminated the training table and encouraged faculty control over athletics — in direct contrast to the eastern schools, which had allowed students to manage their athletic programs throughout the nineteenth century.

The sudden faculty intrusion reflected an early concern for safety and an element of general altruism. The explanation offered by Captain Palmer E. Pierce of West Point, who noted that college professors acted to "conserve the educational good of athletics," was, in this respect, typical.[12] While many well-intentioned individuals acted for this reason, one can base another plausible explanation for faculty control on the self-interest of the faculty members themselves.

At first, one might assume that faculty members sought control over college athletics because they coveted the revenue sports generated. During this time, however, college athletics generated insignificant amounts of money; large stadiums were rare, and admission fees, when charged, were relatively low. Instead of seeking to garner revenue, the faculty may have finally noted the valuable publicity sports had begun to produce.

A successful team saw its exploits printed in all the major newspapers and magazines (and later broadcast on the radio). While a superior academic department received little notice beyond educational circles, the nation's top college football teams had begun to receive national publicity. The publicity promoted the name and the image of a school, theoretically inducing more students to attend and more alumni to feel a warm, lucrative pride in their alma mater. This increase in enrollment and contributions might preserve faculty jobs and even promote the expansion of the university and its faculty. The faculty, therefore, had large and immediate incentives to control college athletics and encourage the team's success.

Casual support for this rather cynical explanation comes from the fact that midwestern instead of eastern schools first instituted faculty control. Older, established, and generally perceived as providing a fine education, the eastern schools had little trouble attracting students and had little need for the publicity college football provided. Schools in the Midwest, however, had neither the reputations nor the traditions of the eastern schools, and they had more difficulty attracting students. Hence the faculties at these schools were the first willing to involve themselves in college sports oversight.

Additional support for this interpretation comes from an article written by an anonymous faculty athletic adviser:

A large factor in promoting this win-at-any-price policy of many college administrations is the newspaper attention given to winning teams and to individual stars.... This willingness to give space to winning athletics coupled with the difficulty of getting adequate reporting of other phases of college life, campus scandal excepted, is the basis for the calculated use of athletics as an advertising medium.[13]

Chancellor James R. Day of Syracuse University made a similar observation:

There are institutions that will not play or row with some other colleges whom they fear, because if beaten it would hurt their prestige and decrease the advertising value of their team or crew.[14]

Thus, a cynical explanation for the faculty takeover of college athletics is that faculties had begun to realize that they could use college sports to promote their colleges and universities.

FOOTBALL VIOLENCE AND A
NEW ATHLETIC ASSOCIATION

Meanwhile, between 1890 and 1905 different coalitions organized a variety of rules committees, causing a great deal of confusion among teams that often had to learn two or more sets of rules to play intercollegiate football. But even with these attempts at standardization, football remained a brutal game characterized by flying wedges, primitive strategy, and dangerous equipment. The public gradually began to protest this brutal violence until, in 1905, some official response to the outcry became both expedient and politically beneficial.

More specifically, by the middle of the 1905 season, public criticism of football prompted President Theodore Roosevelt to invite representatives of Yale, Harvard, and Princeton to the White House to discuss rule changes that would encourage football safety. The meeting between the president and D. H. Nichols and W. T. Reid of Harvard, Arthur Hildenbrand and John B. Fines of Princeton, and Walter Camp and Walter Owsley of Yale took place on October 19, 1905.[15] Another meeting between President Roosevelt and W. T. Reid and Herbert White of Harvard occurred on December 4, 1905, at a White House luncheon. Shortly after this second meeting, the president publicly directed these three eastern universities to save the game. "Brutality and foul play," he advised them, "should receive the same summary punishment given to a man who cheats at cards."[16]

Roosevelt's involvement with football seemed natural, given his hardy, outdoorsman image. A 135-pound boxer while attending Harvard, he encouraged young men to engage in "rough sports which called for pluck, endurance, and physical address."[17] During this period of public displeasure toward football violence, Roosevelt was called on by football's opponents and supporters alike to champion their respective causes, but he refused. He did not waver, even when his son, Theodore, Jr., a freshman at Harvard, was injured in the Harvard-Yale freshman football game in 1905. Theodore, Jr., suffered cuts and bruises and a broken nose, prompting his father to write that he was glad "you played football this year, and I am not at all sorry you are too light to try out for the varsity."[18]

Roosevelt's public instruction to the three Ivy League schools no doubt encouraged football enthusiasts, but the largest stimulus surely came from two near fatal injuries and a death that occurred on the gridiron late in the 1905 season. On November 25, 1905, Harold Moore of Union College died during a football game with New York University. The coroner's report later showed that his "death ensued from a fracture of the skull, sustained . . . in the impact with a single player."[19] Added to Moore's death was the fact that Captain Hurley of Harvard and Douglas Carter of Columbia had sustained serious injuries only a short time before that. In all, the 1905 football season had left 18 dead and 159 with "more or less serious injuries."[20]

Reacting to this violence and the public controversy, Chancellor Day of Syracuse observed that "one human life is too big a price for all the games of the season."[21] Henry L. MacCraken, chancellor of New York University, declared that "the game should be abolished for a term of years, at least."[22] MacCraken's own university, however, ignored his advice.

Uptown, Columbia University President Nicholas M. Butler called football "brutal and abominable."[23] At the end of the 1905 season, Columbia did, in fact, abolish football and did not resume intercollegiate play for ten years. In the Midwest, Northwestern and Union suspended football for one year, while in the West, California and Stanford dropped it, choosing instead to play rugby.

In short, the need to change the rules of football to make the game safe had become obvious, but it remained unclear who should enact the changes. The old rules committee and the various ad hoc alliances appeared incapable of making adequate revisions; in fact, Columbia's Butler labeled the old rules committee "self-perpetuating, irresponsible, impervious to public opinion and culpable" for having failed to install better safeguards in the game.[24]

Harvard's President Charles W. Eliot was asked to take charge of the rules changes, but refused, citing a "lack of jurisdiction."[25] Chancellor MacCraken of New York University finally took the initiative and invited representatives from 19 colleges and universities to discuss the problems plaguing football. MacCraken, a proponent of abolition, outlined in advance three overriding questions:

1. Should football be abandoned?
2. If not, what reforms are necessary to eliminate its objectionable features?
3. If so, what substitute would you suggest to take its place?[26]

Representatives of 13 institutions attended the meeting held on December 8, 1905, at the Murray Hill Hotel in New York City. The meeting began with the scheduled debate over abolishment. Columbia, New York University, and Union, the three schools recently touched by death and injury, argued in favor of abolishment. West Point led the profootball side.

In that debate, Captain Palmer E. Pierce characterized football as an excellent test of character and vowed that the U.S. Military Academy (Army) would continue to play the game whether other colleges did or not. Along with Lieutenant Colonel Howze, also of West Point, Pierce dominated the proceedings and after a battle secured a two-thirds vote to continue the game and make changes recommended by the athletic association of West Point.[27] After a majority of the 13 schools decided to retain but reform football, another meeting was scheduled for December 28, 1905, to include all major universities and colleges that played intercollegiate football. It was left for that second meeting to choose a football rules committee to rewrite the rules of the sport and reduce the game's brutality.

Representatives from 62 colleges attended the second meeting, but noticeably absent were delegations from Yale, Harvard, Princeton, the University of Chicago, Cornell, University of Pennsylvania, and the

U.S. Naval Academy (Navy), the institutions that had formed the reigning rules committee (hereafter referred to as the old rules committee).

One section of the enlarged group wanted to form a new, distinct, completely separate rules committee. Others felt the new committee should incorporate the old committee. After extended debate, the attendees established a seven-man committee and directed it to align, if possible, with the old committee to establish rules that curtailed football violence. If it could not coordinate with the old committee, the new committee was instructed to organize a separate set of rules designed to

1. open the game;
2. eliminate rough and brutal play;
3. achieve efficient enforcement of rules, making the rules definite and precise in all respects such as definitions of brutal play, holding, and tripping; and
4. organize a permanent body of officials.[28]

The conference also adopted a resolution that condemned as unworthy and dishonorable universities (1) offering inducements to athletes to enter their schools, (2) using nonamateurs, and (3) deliberately attempting to injure opposing players.[29]

This group of 62 schools called itself the Intercollegiate Athletic Association of the United States (IAAUS) and elected Palmer E. Pierce of West Point its first president. It appointed an executive committee, assigned it to prepare a constitution, and concluded its meeting by agreeing to meet again in one year unless the president should call an earlier meeting.

PREVENTING INJURIES THROUGH COLLECTIVE ACTION

While the establishment of the IAAUS in 1905 probably saved college football, the question remains why the response to the systematic physical injury and even death on college athletic fields was the formation of an academic consortium rather than unilateral action. One answer comes from examining the college football market.

Although violence may have been an unfortunate concomitant of the sport, football was not, overall, a market failure. The cost of violence was internalized by those who accepted the risk of playing an inherently dangerous game. It was part of the "choice calculus" a college football player made. While the establishment of the IAAUS and the subsequent regulation of intercollegiate sports may have appeared at the time a logical response to brutality, it is, on closer inspection, an odd response coming from an enlightened segment of society. However, from an economist's viewpoint, a far more plausible explanation for the formation of the IAAUS comes from examining the conflict in incentives facing a firm (a football-playing school) and its industry (intercollegiate athletics) and observing the presence of an intraindustry externality: violence resulting in injury.

Individual schools had a large incentive to continue the violent play because of the favorable publicity a winner attracted. This desire to win games and achieve prominence led to more violence and death.

Collectively, at the industry level, cooler heads saw that if all schools resorted to dangerous techniques, not only would the distasteful mayhem continue, but demand for the product would drop as well. Ironically, the game became boring when roughness replaced prowess. Thus, the more brutality, the lower the demand for the industry's product.

This incentive conflict produced an industrywide externality. If one school used violent techniques, it prospered at the expense of those who both lost and bore the image of a loser. If all schools used dangerous techniques, demand fell and everyone lost. The obvious way to remedy the problem was for everyone to abjure violent techniques, but no school would do this unilaterally because it would find itself at a competitive disadvantage.

It may seem strange to a modern reader used to the stylized brutality of the National Football League to hear that as football became more violent in the early 1900s, it also lost interest for spectators. But Frank W. Nicolson, secretary of the Association, observed this trend in his 1912 report to the annual convention:

[E]ven [football's] enthusiastic supporters began to admit that it was losing its former thrills. Not infrequently it happened that the lovers of the sport left the field before the end of the game, wearied by the monotonous series of mass play.... Not only was the game deadly in its dreariness, but ... it was growing more deadly to the participants.[30]

To solve this incentive problem, a body with industrywide representation (the IAAUS) finally established a uniform set of rules to govern the sport. These standardized rules prevented injuries by outlawing the rougher tactics, and, when all schools recognized the authority of the IAAUS and agreed to abide by its rules, they solved the conflict of incentives. The standardized rules eliminated the incentive to use rough techniques because schools that used a safer style of play no longer relinquished an advantage. Moreover, the safer rules provided a better product, which more people wanted to watch.

Unlike the early, short-lived football associations, the IAAUS from the start held the promise of durability. By 1905 schools were finally forced to address the problem of injuries in college football, a problem the early athletic associations largely overlooked. This sudden cooperation is perfectly consistent with the predictions of economic theory.

When an industry seeks to address an intraindustry externality, individual firms tend to resist if they perceive the benefit of addressing the problem to be less than the cost. But once they see this formula reversed, firms become eager to address an intraindustry externality. If schools had drawn up a set of binding rules in, for example, 1890, the benefit (fewer injuries) would have been lower than the cost (an inability to use a skill that led reliably to winning). By 1905, however, the benefits of addressing the injury problem (the continuation of the sport, a livelier game, fewer injuries) outweighed the cost (curtailment of rough play).

Another sign that the IAAUS was destined to enjoy more success than its predecessors was its membership. Most of the earlier athletic bodies had been run by students, and because the membership changed so frequently, long-range planning was difficult. The IAAUS, by contrast, was composed primarily of faculty members and official representatives of the competing institutions. These members brought a more mature attitude to the Association and a more stable presence. Furthermore, the Association's first elected president, Captain Palmer E. Pierce, a professional military officer schooled in discipline and organization, provided better leadership than any other association had experienced.

While by 1906 those who ran football back on campus may not have had complete control over all aspects of intercollegiate football, they finally had an organization within which they could meet, draw up standard rules, and contemplate how to increase their growing influence. The way in which they proceeded to increase and consolidate this influence explains later evolutions in the regulation of nearly all of college athletics. Once colleges organized to police safety and standardize the industry's product, it would become relatively easy for them to promulgate other types of athletic regulations.

STRUCTURE OF THE EARLY NCAA

Membership and Fees

The Association's first constitution stipulated that "all colleges and universities in the United States are eligible for membership" with the understanding that each must agree to the Association's standards of athletic conduct and to confront abuses in college sports. A $25 membership fee defrayed "the necessary expense of officers, committees, and of administration."[31] An institution that paid this fee became an active member entitled to one vote on all motions before each annual convention.

In 1908, the Association established a joint membership category in which two or more colleges or universities agreed to divide the membership fee and to be represented by one delegation. The delegation membership was divided among participating schools, but a joint member had only one vote. In 1909, the IAAUS established the associate membership category open to any "institution of learning" other than a college or university. Prominent associate members included high schools, athletic clubs, conferences, and associations. Associate members paid a $10 fee, could send a delegation to annual conventions, but could not vote. Between 1910—the year the IAAUS changed its name to the National Collegiate Athletic Association—and 1922, there were no membership revisions in the constitution.

In 1922, however, three membership categories were established: active, allied, and associate. Active membership was open to all those colleges and universities that paid the $25 membership fee and subscribed to the rules of the Association. Active members were entitled to send a delegation of no more than three representatives to the annual convention. This delegation had one vote to cast on all NCAA issues.

Allied membership, a category that replaced the joint membrship, included various athletic conferences. Initially, allied members paid no dues, but in 1924 they too were required to pay $25. The fee was waived, however, if a majority of the conference members already belonged to the NCAA. Allied members were also allowed a three-person delegation and one vote at the conventions.

An associate membership, similar to that category established 13 years earlier, was open to groups organized for the purpose of conducting sports competition. Associate members had their $10 membership fee waived if a majority of the group were already NCAA members and were represented at the convention by a nonvoting delegation. No further revisions in membership took place until 1941, by which time the membership reached 252.

The 1941 convention brought constitutional changes that divided the membership into the four categories that exist today: active, allied, associate, and affiliated. The first three categories retained the characterizations and followed the requirements specified in the 1922 constitution; the affiliated included "groups and associations intimately related to intercollegiate athletics in their functioning and purposes, but failing by their nature to qualify for other classes of membership."[32] An affiliated member paid no dues, was not entitled to vote, but could send a one-person delegation to all conventions.

Thus, a series of constitutional revisions completed by 1941 adopted a complex NCAA membership policy that encouraged the Association's expansion. The NCAA's ability to increase its membership contrasts with the desultory, generally unsuccessful attempts of the nineteenth century athletic associations to attract any stable membership at all. How the NCAA succeeded so dramatically in increasing its membership requires further examination of its membership fees.

One immediately apparent attraction was the NCAA's pricing policy, with the flexibility to attract a broad membership. At first, all schools had to pay a $25 fee, but as Paul Stagg discovered while researching the NCAA's early years, this fee, which now sounds so modest, discouraged some schools from joining.[33] Since we know that individuals tend to engage in certain activities when the benefits exceed the costs, those institutions that failed to join the early NCAA considered the benefits of membership less than the $25 cost.

The multitiered pricing structure eventually adopted by the NCAA presents evidence of possible price discrimination. By charging higher prices to schools with extensive sports programs and lower fees to schools with smaller programs, the Association did, as economic theory predicts, increase membership and revenue. The possibility of more than one school joining under a single membership, however, casts doubt on the idea that the NCAA actively used price discrimination to enhance its financial situation.

The joint and later allied membership, which allowed two or more schools to join the Association as one, imposed no restrictions on the number of institutions that could join in this category. This generous requirement allowed a large number of schools to join, each school paying only part of one fee. For example, by joining the Association as a joint member in 1921, the entire 18-college Kansas Intercollegiate Athletic Conference paid only one $25 fee instead of separate fees totaling $450. Had the NCAA followed a strict revenue maximization policy, large joint memberships like these, which represented considerable lost income, would not have existed.

One can reconcile the inexpensive memberships by observing that the NCAA could expect many members to purchase NCAA rule books and to participate in the NCAA tournaments and championships already becoming popular. Because these organized competitions generated substantial revenue, more NCAA members meant more competitors and a better contest that more fans would pay to see. The understanding that more members translated into more revenue through the purchase of other NCAA-controlled products suggests the complexity of the NCAA's revenue-generating mechanism and supports the idea that the NCAA designed its membership policy to maximize revenue from the beginning.

Between 1909 and 1922, membership increased significantly (almost doubling), while the total annual membership fees received rose only from $1,675 to $2,610 during this period.[34] Consequently, even if this membership increase had been solely in response to the Association's fee structure, the increase was not yet substantial. But by the early 1920s, after relying on membership dues in its first ten years of existence to finance all its endeavors, the Association discovered that it could make large sums on NCAA-sponsored athletic events and tournaments.[35] Thus, the revenue sacrificed by allowing several schools to join under one membership fee could be easily made up by the revenue the NCAA collected in tournaments, rule book sales, and the like.

The NCAA's membership policy was, of course, more complex than simply increasing members so as to increase revenue. To establish the authority to change and standardize sports rules, the NCAA had to prove that it represented a large majority of competing colleges and universities, and the best proof lay in impressive membership figures. With a large membership, and the credibility it implied, the NCAA could convince those who played the sports whose rules they rewrote that it possessed the authority to make the rule revisions.

To achieve this credibility, the NCAA actively courted the schools that comprised the old rules committee: Harvard, Yale, Pennsylvania, Chicago, Cornell, Princeton, and Navy. Their membership would sanction the Association and reinforce its power to change the rules. The Association also encouraged high schools and athletic clubs to join by establishing special membership categories and prices for each.

Since any new group or club naturally seeks to increase its membership, this last point may at first seem trivial. But the NCAA, more than merely a club, was a group seeking to regulate college sports. Unlike other regulatory agencies with the legal power to enforce compliance, the NCAA could force no one to adopt its rules. To rout the "dangerous elements" from a sport, it not only had to establish rules that promoted safety, but it also had to win acceptance for these rules among all who played that sport. This need for voluntary compliance placed the NCAA in a difficult situation. Hence, a policy designed to make NCAA membership attractive was also an attempt to persuade schools to acquiesce in the NCAA's decision-making power.

Practices uncannily successful in raising the membership inevitably helped establish the NCAA as a national sports body. By 1941, the

Association could claim that its decisions carried the approval of 252 members, a large membership that directly increased the NCAA's revenue and lent sanction to all NCAA activities. This large membership, which included a majority of colleges and universities that maintained athletic programs, also provided the prerequisites for NCAA policies that would soon restrict the actions of the producers of athletic contests and the wages they paid their student-athletes.

NCAA Officers

Though the Association had elected a president, vice-president, and secretary-treasurer in 1905 without a constitution, its first constitution in 1906 made these positions official. That constitution provided each officer with a one-year term, with elections at the annual convention. Any vacancy during the year would be filled by the Executive Committee.

The early constitution gave each officer specific but limited power. The president would preside over the meetings of the Association's Executive Committee. The vice-president would act as president if the president were absent. The secretary-treasurer would keep records of all meetings, report the minutes, and take charge of all funds.

The 1906 constitution also allowed the president to appoint a nominating committee that would select nominees for an executive committee. These nominees, plus others offered from the floor, were to be chosen by the entire Association and would become the Executive Committee. The Executive Committee conducted the work of the Association between meetings through correspondence and with proper notification to the secretary-treasurer. It also met the evening before the annual convention to consider the agenda for the meeting.

The first two Executive Committees consisted of four representatives from the Northeast, the Midatlantic region, the Midwest, and the South. In 1908, revisions in the constitution provided for the expansion of the Executive Committee to six members, still representing specific geographic districts. The Association continually redivided the United States, causing the number of the districts on the Executive Committee to grow to seven in 1911, eight in 1912, and nine in 1916. Constitutional changes in 1924 consolidated two districts, returning the number of district representatives on the Executive Committee to eight.[36]

Membership in the Executive Committee, however, kept growing even after the number of district representatives stabilized, mainly because the 1910 changes in the constitution allowed one member from each local league or conference of colleges whose membership consisted of at least seven colleges, four or more of them being members of the association, to be on the Executive Committee.[37] To solve the problem of the Executive Committee becoming too large to function effectively, the Council of the NCAA (hereafter simply "the Council") replaced the Executive Committee in 1922 as the Association's governing body.

Charged with governance and general direction of the association, the Council consisted of representatives from each geographical district (then nine, reduced to eight two years later), five members-at-large, the president, and the secretary-treasurer, the last two ex officio members. The members at large allowed athletic conferences to be represented, but unlike the revisions of 1910, their numbers were limited. At the same time the NCAA formed a new Executive Committee, composed of five members from the Council to serve one-year terms under the direction and general instruction of the Council.[38]

Other 1922 revisions included the elimination of one vice-president in favor of eight vice-presidents, the eight district representatives. All vice-presidents were empowered to represent the president in their respective districts and arbitrate possible violations of the principles of amateurism. Each was charged with "observing and supervising the conduct of intercollegiate sports in his district."[39] All were authorized to appoint three or more assistants (an Advisory Committee) to help perform these duties.

Constitutional changes in 1922 required each vice-president to present a report at the annual convention covering:

The degree of strictness with which the provisions of the constitution and by-laws and the existing eligibility rules have been enforced during the year;

Modifications or additions to the eligibility code made by institutions, individually or concertedly;

Progress toward uniformity in the conduct of sports and the activities of intercollegiate athletic associations and local athletic conferences or leagues.[40]

No further revisions in the constitution concerning the officers took place until 1928, when the Association expanded the number of members-at-large on the Council and the size of the Executive Committee from five to seven and detailed more precisely the functions of the Executive Committee. These revisions provided the Executive Committee with more authority to conduct the Association's business.

The 1928 NCAA convention charged the Executive Committee with "representing the Council and [empowered it] to transact the business and direct the affairs of the Association between conventions."[41] The Executive Committee had the power to adopt the Association's budget for the fiscal year; appoint the Committee to Nominate Officers, which, in turn, nominated the Association's officers; and appoint the Committee on Committees, which chose nominees for the various rules committees.

Nothing in the development of the Association's governing mechanism during this early period strikes one as unusual. Most clubs elect a president, a vice-president, and a secretary-treasurer. Furthermore, the early (1910) objective of the NCAA to "maintain [athletics] on an ethical plane in keeping with the dignity and high purpose of education" would certainly justify the formation of rules committees to ensure safety. But the increase in the number of vice-presidents and the development of the smaller governing bodies like the Council and Executive Committee deserve additional attention.

The establishment in 1922 of eight vice-presidents to arbitrate purported NCAA rule violations seems to indicate that the Association had begun to allocate its policing on a regional basis. A cartel, as we recall from the Introduction, requires a monitoring mechanism to prevent cheating among its members, and these eight regional monitors provide the first hint of the NCAA's ultimate goal in college sports: the cartelization of intercollegiate athletics. If the Association truly sought a limited role in intercollegiate athletics, why establish such an extensive mechanism to control eligibility?

Why, one might also ask, would the Association set up such an elaborate governing mechanism? Perhaps the NCAA really did need these smaller groups like the Council and the Executive Committee to carry out its official objective efficiently, but a more plausible explanation lies with the inherent expense of decision making in large groups.

As the NCAA membership increased, the Association found it difficult to reach decisions at conventions with a large and often disputant group present. Consequently, the issues the Association voted on tended increasingly toward the noncontroversial. To conduct business, the NCAA had to turn to such smaller, less expensive, more efficient groups as the Council and the Executive Committee.

Meanwhile, to deal with the increase in its size, the NCAA created additional governing bodies. The various sports rules committees still reported to the entire convention, but between annual conventions they worked with the Council and Executive Committee. The vice-presidents and these two bodies exerted a large influence over the agenda of each convention. This historical analysis explains the emergence of the Council, the Executive Committee, and the eight vice-presidents as the embodiment of the NCAA's effort to control a growing bureaucracy and to decrease its decision-making costs.

But economic theory indicates that a reduction in decision-making costs increases the decisions made. Accordingly, once the NCAA instituted an inexpensive decision-making process, one would expect it to use this mechanism, which is to say, to increase its decision making. The establishment of the Council, Executive Committee, and eight vice-presidents, therefore, marked a major change in the philosophy of the NCAA. They enabled it to present comparatively simple issues before its meetings while rendering the intricate and controversial matters more or less in camera.[42]

NCAA Functions

Among the NCAA's first official acts was the establishment of the Football Rules Committee, a seven-man group instructed to rewrite the rules of college football to eliminate dangerous techniques. Because the committee that had written the rules before 1905 remained intact, the NCAA's Football Rules Committee became known as the "new rules committee." The old committee refused to join the NCAA in 1905, and their refusal provided intercollegiate football with two competing rules committees. Foreseeing this embarrassment, the NCAA authorized its rules committee to seek an alignment with the old committee before setting off to write a separate set of rules.

The new committee went to Philadelphia on December 29, 1905, to meet with the old committee to discuss a merger. But the old committee refused to affiliate with the new committee without instructions from their schools, and the affiliation was delayed until mid-January, 1906, when the seven old committee schools received the necessary authorization. On January 12, 1906, a 14-man joint Football Rules Committee (7 each from the old and new committees) formed and appointed four subcommittees, each devoted to studying specific aspects of football.

Members of the old committee, understandably reluctant to share control with the new committee, had no real alternative. Because the old committee had ruled more by influence than coercion, a breakdown in its ability to influence left it with little power to affect the rules of the sport.

The old committee had experienced a decline in its ability to influence other colleges for two reasons. First, it had presided over football during the violent period, and other schools hesitated to trust reform to a committee apparently incapable of ensuring safety in the sport. Second, schools other than the seven belonging to the old committee saw it as an elite group averse to outside advice.

With the influence of the old Football Rules Committee on the wane and with the apparent willingness of the NCAA to establish a new rules system, the old committee saw the logic in affiliation. Combined with the NCAA's Football Rules Committee, the old committee at least shared control over the rules more schools (62 compared with the 7) appeared ready to follow. Moreover, the new Association enjoyed a larger span of influence and was more open to suggestions.

Between 1905 and 1920 the old and new rules committees held several joint meetings with the new rules committee, reporting changes to the annual convention of the NCAA. Gradually, the distinction between the two disappeared as members of the old committee joined the Association.[43] When Navy, the remaining member of the old rules committee, joined the NCAA in 1920, the old rules committee officially dissolved. In 1921, the Association reduced the number of members on its Football Rules Committee to 12 and limited the representatives to terms ranging from one to three years.[44] By 1927, when the membership decided to elect 1 member of the Football Rules Committee from each district to provide a broader representation, any influence the original 7 members of the old committee still had on the rules of football ended.

The Football Rules Committee studied the sport and recommended changes in procedures to be voted on at each annual convention. The recommendations adopted by the entire Association included a standardization of rules, the prohibition of dangerous techniques, the monitoring of officials, and the endorsement of certain kinds of equipment. The rules changes reduced the deaths in college football considerably, with the exception of 1931 and 1932, when a series of deaths traced to intercollegiate football brought quick changes in the rules and equipment. On the whole, though, injuries never again reached the worrisome, pre-1905 proportions after the NCAA began standardizing the rules.

Having established its Football Rules Committee, the NCAA began to consider the possibility of standardizing the rules in other college sports, and in each case, it followed a similar procedural pattern. Initially, it formed a committee to study a particular sport and report on its administration and rules. On the basis of the committee's report, which invariably concluded that the sport could be administered more effectively, the NCAA officially appointed its own rules committee and instructed it to reorganize the rules of the sport. In this way, the NCAA established rules committees in basketball (1908), track and field (1910), soccer (1911), swimming (1913), wrestling (1917), volleyball (1918), boxing (1919), ice hockey (1923), gymnastics (1927), baseball (1928), lacrosse (1929), fencing (1932), golf (1935), and tennis (1937).

Had the NCAA stopped at this point, short of expanding beyond rule writing, the most plausible explanation for its formation would be as an effort to address the problems that stemmed from the absence of standardized sports rules. But the NCAA carried its functions further. Shortly after its formation, it began considering player eligibility, scheduling, and the inducements schools could offer athletes to attend. At first, the actions the NCAA took on these subjects were nothing more than unenforceable resolutions or recommendations. Eventually, however, the Association began actively and coercively to enforce its rules. In considering how the NCAA grew from a body that merely formulated rules to a body that now regulates practically all aspects of college sports, it is important to understand this transition period.

In this early era, the NCAA placed enforcement responsibility on the individual colleges and universities. While most schools agreed in principle to the statutes that outlined the types of appropriate behavior in college athletics, few actively enforced them. An examination of NCAA activities before World War II reveals that once the schools saw that the true cost of these rule violations was fierce competition in the form of expensive and unrestrained student-athlete recruitment, they also saw how they would all benefit if this competition were restrained.

This problem derived from the different incentives an individual firm (a school) and the industry (college athletics) faced. Once an NCAA resolution was passed, each school had an incentive not to enforce it—to obtain, instead, an advantage by not restricting its behavior the way its competitors presumably were. If all schools reacted to an incentive this way, each spent resources competing while none obtained an advantage. If the divergent incentive problem could be solved by making it difficult for schools to violate NCAA agreements, all the "firms" in the industry would benefit by conserving resources otherwise expended in fruitless competition. Accordingly, once the members of the Association recognized the incentive problem within intercollegiate athletics, their reluctance to enact enforceable rules ended.

In its pre-World War II period, the NCAA discovered this incentive problem by passing resolutions that were consistently violated. Finally, the Association realized that the breakdown in behavior was less the fault of the resolutions than a natural reaction to the lack of adequate enforcement. An examination of the NCAA's first efforts to control the eligibility of student-athletes dramatizes the frustrations with "free riding" that helped direct the Association toward active enforcement practices.

THE NCAA'S AMATEUR CODE

The Amateur Code the NCAA drew up shortly after its formation represented its first statement on the subject of player eligibility, one of the first nonrule questions it studied. The Association initially considered the question of eligibility for graduate students and decided to prohibit postgraduate participation. It also considered participation of amateurs and professionals in college sports, and the first NCAA statement regarding the amateur-professional question appeared in the 1906 constitution. In the section entitled "Principles of Amateur Sports," the NCAA declared itself in favor of amateur participation and against the following:

> The offering of inducements to players to enter colleges or universities because of their athletic abilities and of supporting or maintaining players while students on account of their athletic abilities, either by athletic organizations, individual alumni, or otherwise, directly or indirectly.
>
> The singling out of prominent athletic students of preparatory schools and endeavoring to influence them to enter a particular college or university.[45]

During the NCAA's first six years, several of its committees studied amateurism, and these committees adopted various definitions of *amateurism* and *professionalism*. According to the NCAA's Committee on Amateurism of 1912:

> An amateur in athletics is one who enters and takes part in athletic contests purely in obedience to the play impulse or for the satisfaction of purely play motives and for the exercise, training, and social pleasures derived. The natural or primary attitude of mind and motives in play determines amateurism.
>
> A professional in athletics is one who enters or takes part in athletic contests for any other motive than the satisfaction of pure play impulses or for the exercise, training, and social pleasures derived, or one who desires and secures from his skill or who accepts of spectators, partisan or other interest, any material or economic advantage or reward.[46]

(Many casual observers believe that the NCAA endorsed the participation of amateurs to keep intercollegiate athletics "pure," but we cannot ignore the fact that it was cheaper to allow amateur rather than professional participation.[47] A cynical interpretation of this act, therefore, might be that the NCAA prohibited payment to athletes to cut "production cost" in the mistaken belief that they could prohibit the payments and preclude professionalism by merely passing a resolution.)

To augment its Amateur Code, the NCAA also formalized rules of eligibility. Previously, skilled athletes often traveled from school to school, participating in athletics at each institution.[48] Before the NCAA, some athletic conferences had addressed the problems of the "tramp athlete" by establishing rules prohibiting freshmen from playing (the one-year freshman rule), limiting participation (the three-year participation rule), requiring a student to be enrolled for a minimum number of credits, and preventing a student from participating in athletics for a year if he transferred to another school (the one-year transfer rule). The NCAA's first eligibility code combined sections of these early codes, but it most closely resembled the code of the Western Conference (Big Ten), which had established one of the most thorough codes in the country. (The NCAA's first Eligibility Code appears as Appendix A.)

Having made a major investment to develop codes covering amateurism and eligibility, the NCAA expended almost no time or effort to ensure that its codes were followed. It appears, in fact, that the Association never expected to enforce these codes itself. Rather, it thought it could rely on each school, conference, or league to police amateurism and eligibility. This decentralized enforcement did not reduce the number of violations, because the schools, conferences, and leagues did little to enforce the codes, and during this time (the middle of the second decade) the NCAA discovered its diverging incentive problem. Continually condemning violators of the Amateur and Eligibility Codes, the Association went on continually encountering violations. Oddly enough, the sport that gave the NCAA the most difficulty in this regard was college baseball.

Even though baseball already enjoyed an established set of rules, the NCAA chose to exert its control over the rules of intercollegiate baseball and chose to focus on the less settled problem of professionalism. The Association quickly discovered that with the widespread organization of professional and semiprofessional baseball in the early 1900s, it was not unusual for a baseball player to have played for pay before college. By 1917, so many college students were playing summer professional baseball that, of the 137 colleges insisting upon amateurism in sports, 105 permitted baseball players to compete in professional summer leagues.[49]

While summer baseball provided the most flagrant violation of the codes, reports of violations in other sports increased in the second decade of the twentieth century. In 1912, a survey on college athletic administration, conducted by NCAA Secretary-Treasurer Frank W. Nicolson, found that 27 percent of the schools enforced the one-year freshman rule while 10 percent of the schools enforced less stringent residence requirements. The survey also reported that about 60 percent of all schools prohibited graduate students from participating in college athletics and fewer than 50 percent barred professional students. Finally, the survey revealed that less than 60 percent of the institutions enforced the one-year transfer rule.[50]

By the end of World War I, it was well known that NCAA codes were being ignored. In an effort to solve the enforcement problem, the NCAA revised its constitution at the annual convention of 1921, thereby adopting a considerable change in philosophy. The original constitution stated that the object of the Association "shall be to study various important phases of college athletics, to formulate rules governing athletics, and to promote the adoption of recommended measures." The 1921 constitutional changes expanded on the generally altruistic original purposes of the NCAA, but three new Association objectives were added that showed the NCAA moving more toward the detailed regulation of the conditions of intercollegiate athletic participation. These new objectives of the Association were as follows:

The establishment of a uniform law of amateurism and of principles of amateur sports.

The encouragement of the adoption by its constituent members of strict eligibility rules to comply with high standards of scholarship, amateur standing, and good sportsmanship.

The supervision of regulations, and conduct, by its constituent members, of intercollegiate sports and regional and national amateur athletic contests, and the preservation of collegiate athletic records.[51]

The Association went still further to advocate the principles of amateurism by amending its constitution to specify the members' views on amateurism. To raise its Amateur Code higher among its policies, the NCAA moved the code out of the bylaws into the main body. Most prominent in the new section was the identification of specific code violations, with particular emphasis on preventing pay or financial compensation for sports participants. The *New York Times* describes these changes as attempts by the NCAA to lift itself "out of the situation under which it has been laboring since birth in 1906 and move it into an up to date working body in which participation and theory are playfellows."[52]

Others, however, saw these revisions as the NCAA's attempt to supersede its original purpose by establishing a system of control over all of college athletics. Princeton, Harvard, Cornell, and the City College of New York, for example, accused the NCAA of seeking more power and threatened to withdraw. NCAA President Pierce responded. The reasons for the changes, he said, were "to enunciate more clearly [the Association's] purposes; to incorporate the amateur definition and principles of amateur spirit; [and] to widen the scope of government."[53]

Some members also questioned the motives of individuals involved, especially Pierce's, suggesting that they sought dictatorial control over the NCAA. Described as "expressing heated resentment that any reflections should be passed upon the motives of those espousing constitutional changes," Pierce revealed that he had asked not to be renominated for the Association's presidency. But despite the controversy, the NCAA adopted its constitutional revisions in late December 1921 and reelected Pierce president.

It was expected that these revisions, by specifically detailing prohibited activities, would solve the divergent incentive problem, but with the lack of an enforcement mechanism, the committee reports between 1922 and 1925 show that the violations continued. Baseball remained the most troubling sport, as (still) President Pierce noted in 1924: "It is to be regretted that all colleges do not unite on a wholehearted and effective effort to prevent their undergraduates playing, without loss of amateur status, baseball for money or its equivalent."[54] Pierce also recognized the absence of enforcement as the major problem confronting the Association. In the same speech he observed, "All members of the National Collegiate Athletic Administration have adopted the Amateur Law; the enforcement of this law, however, is not uniform throughout the country."

No new measures to ensure that members obeyed the Association's regulations appeared between 1921 and 1934, but there was no shortage of resolutions, in general recommending appropriate athletic behavior and specifically

1. condemning the use of students previously employed in professional football,
2. disapproving preseason football practice,
3. organizing committees to investigate amateur violations,
4. condemning postseason bowl games, and
5. seeking to limit the number of regular season football games.

Completely unenforceable, these resolutions had little effect, but they represented an increase in the issues upon which the NCAA passed its judgment. In economic terms, they reveal that the Association was increasingly concerned with the number of contests (output) and the qualifications and the payments made to those who played them (input).

FOUR MAJOR EVENTS SHAPING THE NCAA'S DESTINY BETWEEN 1929 AND 1939

As the 1920s came to a close, the NCAA could confidently attribute its inability to exert control over intercollegiate athletics beyond mere rulemaking to the lack of an effective enforcement mechanism.[55] In the 11 years before World War II, however, four specific events hastened the adoption of just such a mechanism:

1. the 1929 Carnegie Foundation report on amateur college athletics;
2. the Great Depression;
3. the dramatic increase in revenue generated by college sports, which resulted in the federal government's desire to tax admissions, and a proliferation of radio play-by-play broadcasts that began to undermine attendance; and
4. the failure of a comprehensive but voluntary 1934 code on subsidizing and recruiting student-athletes to curtail professionalism.

The Carnegie Foundation Report

In 1916 the NCAA adopted a resolution calling for an independent foundation to study intercollegiate athletics in the United States, and, after several other foundations declined, the Carnegie Foundation undertook the task.[56] Thirteen years later, in 1929, the Foundation finally issued its report, a document that detailed widespread violations of the Amateur Code in college sports. The Carnegie Foundation visited 112 colleges and universities in the United States and Canada to conduct its study, which traced the growth, development, and administration of intercollegiate sports. It reported on the quality of college coaching, the relationship between the press and college athletics, and the values taught by college athletics. But the section that drew the most attention was entitled "The Recruiting and Subsidization of Athletes."[57]

The Carnegie Foundation defined recruiting as "the solicitation of school athletes with a view to inducing them to attend a college or university" and subsidization as

the provision of financial or other assistance to athletes in consideration of their services on school or college teams or squads, whether in the years during which these services were rendered or some other years.[58]

While the NCAA already "recommended against" both recruiting and subsidization, the public revelation by the Carnegie Foundation that the practices were widespread demonstrated to the membership how ineffectively its codes performed.

The Carnegie Foundation reported that recruiting athletes, a direct violation of the NCAA code, was routinely conducted by alumni, athletic coaches, and college fraternities. Recruiting, they found, varied from writing letters describing a particular institution to an athlete to lavish, all-expenses-paid campus visits. The Carnegie Foundation summarized its findings this way:

The recruiting of American college athletes, be it active or passive, professional or non-professional, has reached the proportions of nationwide commerce.... The element that demoralizes is the subsidy, the monetary or material advantage that is used to attract the schoolboy athlete. It is seldom lacking in the general process of gathering a "winning team."[59]

The report also found that subsidization, expressly forbidden by the NCAA, occurred openly at 81 of the 112 institutions studied. The commonest methods of subsidizing athletes were to offer jobs of various kinds, scholarships, or loans.[60] The Carnegie Foundation found that the subsidizing took place in an organized way (within athletic departments) and among unorganized interest groups (like alumni fraternities) and that it was a commonplace occurrence rather than an anachronistic practice, as the NCAA claimed.

The Carnegie Report received considerable publicity, and in the following years newspapers and magazines published many reports and follow-up studies based on it.[61] So large was its impact that Howard Savage, the principal author, was invited to address the NCAA convention in both 1929 and 1930 and to write a series of articles about the NCAA and the report for the *New York Times*.[62]

But as prominent a subject of discussion at the 1929 and 1930 NCAA conventions as the Carnegie Report may have been, the Association took little action to halt rule violations. In 1931, the *New York Times* conducted a survey of NCAA members that revealed how minuscule an effect the Carnegie Report had exerted on intercollegiate athletics. Asked, "What, if any, changes have been manifest since the publication a year ago of the Carnegie Report on subsidizing and recruiting?" two-thirds of the schools replied "none."

The Carnegie Foundation Report demonstrated how ineffectively the NCAA maintained its Amateur and Eligibility Codes, it received considerable publicity, and it preoccupied the members of the Association; nevertheless, it precipitated by itself no official NCAA action designated to decrease violations. It did, however, force the members to confront the enormity of the problem and to plan ways to solve it.

The Great Depression of 1929

The year of the Carnegie Report also marked the beginning of the Great Depression. Throughout the 1920s ticket sales for college sports events had increased steadily, and most of the schools that maintained

athletic programs enjoyed large and relatively sudden revenue in-
flows. Generally, they used this money to fund the so-called minor (non-
revenue-producing) sports and to expand their sports facilities. But the
equally sudden contrary effects of the Depression decreased the
public's willingness to purchase tickets.

College sports felt no direct, substantial effect until 1931, when
revenues from all college sports fell by 15 percent.[63] But by 1933 some
southern schools were reporting cuts in revenue of up to 25 percent.[64]
Some other schools defrayed the decrease in demand by lowering admission prices and were consequently able to report increases in attendance though not in revenue.[65]

The decline in revenue quickly turned the colleges to cost cutting.
For example, in 1931 the University of Iowa eliminated spring baseball
and reduced the number of athletes it took on road trips. Temple
University dropped one football game from its ten-game schedule.[66]
The Universities of Michigan and Minnesota dropped hockey, while
the University of Wisconsin dropped both hockey and crew.[67]

Overall, the Depression forced athletic departments to reduce
schedules, reduce team travel, cut their staffs, and drop some minor
sports. It demonstrated that college athletics was a business dependent upon paying customers. An important and lasting effect of the
Depression on intercollegiate sports was to force the schools to apply
financial analyses previously reserved for more traditional businesses
to athletic departments, in an effort to operate economically.

The Effects of Radio and the Threat of Federal Taxation

Meanwhile, startling technological advances in the 1930s, especially
the overnight popularity of radio, made college sports (mostly football)
accessible to many more people. The schools soon discovered, however, that football broadcasts competed with the games themselves for
the consumer's entertainment dollar. Instead of attending the games
and spending money on food and drink, souvenirs, parking, and so
forth, fans stayed at home and heard the game on the radio.

While some argued that radio broadcasts actually increased attendance by exposing different sports to people who might later pay to
see them, many NCAA members believed that radio cut heavily into
attendance. Professor W. B. Owens of Stanford University expressed
this belief in his 1931 district report:

There is a feeling, fairly widespread, that the broadcasting of games has
made serious inroads on the attendance at football games, and that its effect in
this regard may increase. Thousands of people, it is contended, are coming to

prefer a congenial party before the fireplace in the living room, with the radio bringing the game to them, to a seat in the stands from which to witness the contest. "Radio parties" are becoming popular. Even where the "party" does not enter in, it is contended that thousands who might otherwise have gone to the game have preferred listening in at home, to paying the price for tickets and going to the game.[68]

In spite of the ongoing debate, no uniform, national NCAA policy was adopted to address the radio problem. But many schools believed radio broadcasting decreased attendance and joined together at the local level to ban radio broadcasts. The Southern Conference, which consisted of 23 colleges and universities, decided at the close of the 1931 season to bar football broadcasting until further notice. The Western Conference also opposed putting future games on the air, and the Southwest Conference ruled out all broadcasting except that covered by existing contracts.[69]

The true effect of radio broadcasting on attendance remained unclear in this period. At a 1932 NCAA-sponsored discussion about radio's effect, athletic directors and coaches differed sharply, but presented only anecdotal evidence to support their views.[70] In 1936, a committee of three announced that after a one-year study it could not determine if radio broadcasting adversely affected attendance. Based on this study, the NCAA opted not to establish a national policy on radio broadcasting.

While its immediate effect on sports attendance remained ambiguous, broadcasting showed the members of the NCAA the advantage of taking collective action if they perceived a substantial promise of gain or threat of loss. In contrast to the NCAA's attempts to enforce its Amateur and Eligibility Codes, plagued at the time by diverging-incentive problems and consequent cheating, groups within the Association acted together quite successfully to restrict radio broadcasts.

However, the contrast between the unsuccessful attempts to govern behavior through the Amateur and Eligibility Codes and the successful effort to control radio broadcasting should not strike one as unusual. The Amateur and Eligibility Codes invited violations because it was so difficult to observe violations. But the decision to control radio broadcasts had few violations because they were so easy to detect. Finally—and to repeat—having dealt with radio broadcasts, schools now saw they could act collectively if the benefits were great and the violations observable.

Another example of the NCAA's willingness to act collectively when money became the primary motivation arose in the 1930s when the Association organized a special committee to deal with the federal tax levied on admissions to college sports contests. The Federal Revenue Act of 1932 had been amended so that admission to college sports events could be taxed. The NCAA considered the tax, as applied to state-supported institutions, to be unconstitutional, and it prepared test cases to challenge the laws in which certain member schools withheld the tax revenue so that the government had to initiate court action.

After several intermediate cases (which is to say victories for the defendant schools), the federal government appealed to the Supreme Court, which reversed all the lower court decisions. Regardless of the outcome, however, the NCAA had demonstrated again that it could organize collective action and even levy the requisite support when the cost of inaction became clear to each member.[71]

The 1934 Code on Recruiting and Subsidizing Athletes

Familiar problems continued to plague the NCAA throughout the 1930s. By 1933, for example, it was apparent that the Amateur and Eligibility Codes, last updated in 1921, were utterly without effect. Consequently, at the annual convention that year, the president appointed a special committee to study recruiting and subsidizing of athletes and to produce a document outlining proper and improper practices. In 1934 the special committee reported a seven-item code that became known as "The NCAA Code on Recruiting and Subsidizing of Athletes." (See Appendix B.) The 1934 convention adopted this new code as the method to distinguish between "legitimate and illegitimate methods of recruiting athletes."[72]

While the new code was being finalized, the secretary of the NCAA mailed questionnaires asking all the members their opinion of the code. Of the 100 respondents, 36 claimed to be enforcing the code, and 38 found themselves unable "conscientiously [to] reply in the affirmative to the question of enforcement."[73] These admissions both confirmed that many members considered the code impossible to enforce and provided the NCAA with another accurate picture (to match the 1929 Carnegie Foundation report) of how ineffective the voluntary enforcement of a code of athletic conduct really was.

The new code was the most extensive set of recruitment and subsidization rules yet compiled by the NCAA in its 29 years. It was adopted with only the mild objection of those members who believed it to be an attempt by the Association to acquire more power, yet it still lacked an adequate enforcement mechanism, and, like its predecessors, it virtually invited violations. As John J. Tigent, President of the University of Florida, told the 1935 Convention:

[An institution] cannot control the actions of alumni and outsiders, many of whom honestly believe that they are promoting the welfare of the institution and of its athletes in providing some kind of material assistance to them in enabling them to get a college education. When an attempt is made to prohibit strictly the acceptance by athletes of any assistance whatsoever for their athletic services, a situation of dishonesty and hypocrisy develops.[74]

The "improved" code of 1934 further highlighted how powerless the NCAA was against student-athlete recruitment and subsidization. No matter how well intentioned its efforts or how sincere its attempts to compel adherence to a particular code, the NCAA could not prevent schools from offering inducements without some form of coercion. The continuing violations in spite of the 1934 code made this clear.

THE NCAA DURING WORLD WAR II

By the beginning of World War II, the NCAA was poised ready to change from a consultative rules committee to a regulatory body with the power to control and discipline constituents. From the moment the NCAA sought to regulate intercollegiate athletics, instead of merely standardizing the rules of sports, it had needed an enforcement mechanism based on coercion. Lacking for some 30 years either the willingness or the power to develop such a mechanism, the Association nevertheless increased its membership and occasionally dealt decisively with potentially damaging decreases in college sports income. It knew—and was told—how widespread violations of its codes were, but not until the war years did it enjoy the power to organize and deploy an enforcement mechanism capable of deterring the behavior it proscribed.

The size and makeup of the membership helps explain why it took the Association so long to gain the power of coercion. At first many large and influential eastern schools perceived the NCAA as just another transitory athletic association and ignored it. Gradually, however, the membership increased until almost all schools with major athletic programs and many with smaller programs were enrolled. With size came first respectability, then influence, and finally power. Had it tried to coerce members before it spoke for a majority, the NCAA would have failed in much the same way a minority union with little power to retaliate fails to sway management.

At the 1939 annual convention, the NCAA made a significant revision in its constitution by adding a new third article entitled "Declaration of Sound Principles and Practices for Intercollegiate Athletics."[75]

The new article raised so many questions and perplexed so many members that the Association prepared explanatory administrative notes that were included with the sections.

The first sections of the new article, "Amateurism," "Control of Athletics," and "Institutional Control," were summations of previous, much discussed NCAA policies. Section four, however, "Aid for Athletes," outlined the proposed awarding and administration of student-athlete financial aid, a subject not seriously discussed by the Association until the late 1930s. Adoption of this section represented a change from the NCAA's previous reluctance to specify the type of financial aid institutions could give athletes. Heretofore the NCAA had merely asserted that all athletes should be amateurs and had allowed each institution to determine what an amateur might receive. The constitutions used throughout the 1930s included examples of amateur violations, but nothing in these constitutions went beyond a general recommendation. This new section contained five subsections, each detailing different aspects of the aid an athlete could expect.

The first subsection stated that students should enjoy no special aid simply because they were athletes. The NCAA went on to explain that "if a boy's need is established, he should be entitled to aid. On the other hand, if his financial status is such that he or his family can afford to pay for his college education, he should be required to do so."[76]

The second subsection suggested that all such aid to athletes be awarded by the institution's financial aid office. The third subsection ensured that aid would not be taken from an athlete if he discontinued his participation in sports, fearing that such a practice would too closely resemble the "pros." A fourth subsection detailed the conditions whereby an athlete could receive aid from a source other than a relative or guardian or an institution. The fifth subsection specified that the wages paid to athletes employed while in school were to be equal to the wages paid to nonathletes who held the same jobs.

The subsections of this new article show just how interested the NCAA had become in the competition among its members for athletic talent. No matter how the NCAA tried to justify or explain a particular subsection, each contained elements designed to limit competition for athletes, to make the allowable competition observable to all competitors, and where observation was inherently difficult, to ensure that either the NCAA or some other organization could determine what an athlete had received from a school.

The restrictions in the first subsection, governing financial aid based on need, represented an attempt to limit competition by preventing schools from bidding for athletes with their financial aid dollars. Under this new rule, if an athlete could not demonstrate need, a school could not offer him financial aid. In this way the NCAA limited the money its schools could spend to field a team.

The fifth subsection governing the wages paid to athletes also limited competition for athletic talent. The NCAA knew full well when it prohibited direct payments to athletes some schools began to compensate them indirectly by employing them at artificially high wages or in a job with no real responsibility (for example, monitoring the growth of the grass in the stadium). Offering this kind of job as an inducement amounted to competition for athletic talent. To avoid this competition, the NCAA logically prohibited athletes from earning extra money this way.

The second and fourth subsections made the money paid to athletes observable in such a way that nonsanctioned recruiting and all subsidization became apparent. This feature allowed the Association to prevent the competition for athletes that took place when alumni or fraternities offered money to induce student-athletes to attend their school. These subsections also placed the cost of ensuring that the agreements were followed on the separate members—specifically, on their financial aid offices. Though the NCAA did arrange to review the financial aid records, the method it first devised to control competition for athletes reveals that it expected most of the monitoring to be done at its institutions.

With the addition of "Declarations of Sound Principles and Practices for Intercollegiate Athletics," the NCAA had begun to enact detailed and far-reaching measures designed to decrease the cost of producing an athletic contest by limiting competition for student-athletes. With the advent of the 1940s, it seemed clear that the NCAA was ready to address the problem of how to control the entire conduct of intercollegiate athletics. But World War II temporarily postponed the introduction of more regulatory measures. The requirements of the U.S. Armed Forces during World War II severely depleted both the athletic and coaching ranks of intercollegiate sports, and during this period the NCAA lacked the personnel to maintain basic administrative functions, let alone expand its influence.

As more athletes joined the service, the NCAA sought to provide a sufficient number of participants to play out the sports schedules and decided to waive temporarily its one-year residency requirement and let freshmen compete at the varsity level. Freshman eligibility allowed intercollegiate athletics to function with a full schedule, at perhaps a lower skill level, and it also gave the NCAA members some experience they could draw on 30 years later when they permanently adopted freshman eligibility.

Beyond the approval of freshman eligibility, little of note happened in intercollegiate athletics during World War II. The United States became so war oriented that in 1943, for the first and only time, the Association cancelled its annual convention. Instead, it relied on the Council for guidance, which met as regularly scheduled that year.

Nevertheless, an interesting contrast appears between the NCAA's behavior during World War II and its behavior during World War I. When the First World War began, several schools immediately dropped or cut their athletic programs. Some even asked the NCAA to declare hand grenade tossing a championship event. During World War II, however, few schools wanted to curtail their programs, and most NCAA efforts in this war period were designated to maintain the schedules. An understanding of why the NCAA behaved differently in these similar situations lies in the change the NCAA underwent between the wars.

If one accepts the casual empiricism this assertion implies, the different behavior during these war periods can be attributed to a change in goals and functions. During World War I, members of the NCAA found the opportunity cost of patriotism and schedule curtailment quite low because college sports generated comparatively little money. But as the Association grew, its members realized so much revenue (and publicity) that even during World War II they sought to sustain it. By the beginning of the Second World War, the NCAA had developed a keen appreciation for the money produced by college sports.

NOTES

1. Howard J. Savage, *American College Athletics*, Carnegie Foundation for the Advancement of Teaching, Bulletin 23 (Boston: Merrymount Press, 1929), 14.

2. Ibid., 16. Soccer in its pure form is generally referred to as football by non-Americans. Thus, a game featuring soccer-like skills at this time would naturally be called football.

3. Allison Danzig, *The History of American Football* (Englewood Cliffs, N.J: Prentice-Hall, 1956), 7-8.

4. The sport of rugby gets its name from the town where it was first played: Rugby, England. Rugby was first played in 1823, and in 1871, a Rugby union formalized the rules of the sport. The set of rules became known as Rugby Union, in contrast to Rugby League. The difference between the two is that Rugby Union, played with 15 players per team, is amateur rugby, while Rugby League, played with 13-man teams, is professional rugby.

5. Amos Alonzo Stagg, in Danzig, *History of American Football*, 11.

6. Paul Stagg, "The Development of the National Collegiate Athletic Association in Relation to Intercollegiate Athletics in the United States" (Ph.D. diss., New York University, 1946), 17.

7. Danzig, *History of American Football*, 14.

8. Ibid., 15.

9. Alexander M. Weyand, *The Saga of American Football* (New York: Macmillan, 1955), 42.

10. Amos Alonzo Stagg, "Touchdown," *Saturday Evening Post*, Oct. 23, 1926, 109.

11. Danzig, *History of American Football*, 493.

12. Frederick W. Luehring, "The National Collegiate Athletic Association," *Health and Physical Education* 18 (December 1947): 707.

13. The Faculty Athletic Advisor, "Commercialism in College Athletics," *School and Society* 16 (July 1, 1922): 9.

14. J. R. Day, "The Function of College Athletics," *Proceedings of the National Collegiate Athletic Association* 4 (Dec. 28, 1909): 35. (Hereafter all references made to *Proceedings of the National Collegiate Athletic Association* will be cited as (year) *NCAA Proceedings*).

15. Paul Stagg, "Development of the NCAA," 29.

16. Danzig, *History of American Football*, 29.

17. Theodore Roosevelt, *The Strenuous Life* (New York: Century, 1902), 156.

18. E. E. Morrison, *The Letters of Theodore Roosevelt*, vol. 5 (Cambridge: Harvard University Press, 1952), 82.

19. "Moore's Death Accidental," *New York Times*, Dec. 5, 1905, 11.

20. Danzig, *History of American Football*, 29.

21. Weyand, *Saga of American Football*, 82.

22. "Football is Abolished by Columbia Committee," *New York Times*, Nov. 29, 1905, 1.

23. Ibid.

24. "Football Conference at the White House," *New York Times*, Dec. 5, 1905, 11.

25. Danzig, *History of American Football*, 29.

26. "Football Conference Will Convene To-day," *New York Times*, Dec. 8, 1905, 7. Those attending were West Point, Syracuse, Rutgers, Wesleyan, Stevens, Lafayette, Haverford, Swarthmore, Columbia, Union, Rochester, Fordham, and New York University.

27. "Army-Navy Game Here, So Academies Decide," *New York Times*, Dec. 9, 1905, 10.

28. "Football Convention Wants One Rule Code," *New York Times*, Dec. 29, 1905, 7.

29. Ibid.

30. Frank W. Nicolson, "Report of the Secretary," 1912 *NCAA Proceedings*. (The IAAUS changed its name to the National Collegiate Athletic Association in 1910.)

31. 1910 *NCAA Proceedings*, 63, 66.

32. 1941 *NCAA Proceedings*, 180.

33. Paul Stagg, "Development of the NCAA," 33. According to Stagg, "It was found that the expense of maintaining membership kept many of the small institutions from joining as well as a few of the large ones."

34. The 1909 membership receipts were obtained by multiplying the number of schools by the appropriate fee. The fees paid in 1922 appear in 1922 *NCAA Proceedings*, 98-100. In 1922, most schools paid these fees, but some were delinquent.

35. In the report of the treasurer in 1922 *NCAA Proceedings*, however, two track meets and the royalties for copublishing football and basketball rules netted $2,659, more than all membership dues.

36. For a list of the states in each district see 1924 *NCAA Proceedings*, 11.

37. 1910 *NCAA Proceedings*, 35.

38. 1927 *NCAA Proceedings*, 106.

39. 1922 *NCAA Proceedings*, 105.

40. Ibid.

41. 1944 *NCAA Proceedings*, 182.

42. Prior to the reorganization of the governing bodies, the Association dealt with more mundane subjects—supporting amateurism and making recommendations on the status of coaches and the conduct of intramural sports. With the smaller bodies controlling the agenda, the NCAA turned to more complex subjects—developing a working definition of amateurism and eligibility, defining proper and improper recruiting tactics, and attempting to penalize rule violators. The smaller bodies allowed these complex subjects to be addressed more efficiently than if they had been considered by the entire Association.

43. Pennsylvania joined in 1906, Chicago in 1907, Harvard in 1908, Princeton in 1913, Yale in 1915, Cornell in 1919, and Navy in 1920.

44. 1921 *NCAA Proceedings*, 63.

45. 1906 *NCAA Proceedings*, 73.

46. 1912 *NCAA Proceedings*, 34.

47. As an example of how some viewed the need to keep college athletics "pure" by using only amateurs, consider the comments made by the Committee on Amateurs:

It long has been recognized that the amateur and the professional spirit in competitive play are directly antagonistic and that whenever the professional spirit has entered into the conduct of any sport, the nature of the sport has been completely changed, its ethical and moral values have disappeared, and its results have become such in some instances as to place it under the ban of the law of the state. (1912 *NCAA Proceedings*, 32).

48. According to one anonymous observer:

I remember the distinct regret with which we once parted with an athlete, a four-sport man, in his junior year. His (or our) misfortune was that in place of continuing his habit of getting drunk in private, he chose to attempt a solo at a village festival when so intoxicated. . . . [W]ithin a week he was captain of the team in a neighboring college, which did not belong to our athletic organization. (The Faculty Athletic Advisor, "Commercialism in College Athletics," *School and Society*, June 24, 1922, 684).

49. 1917 *NCAA Proceedings*, 39.

50. Frank W. Nicolson, "Replies to Questionnaire on College Athletic Administration," *Booklet*, 1912.

51. 1921 *NCAA Proceedings*, 90, 96.

52. "NCAA Decides to Change Status," *New York Times*, Dec. 29, 1922, 10.

53. 1922 *NCAA Proceedings*, 10.

54. 1924 *NCAA Proceedings*, 81.

55. For example, see the report on the NCAA's futile attempts to stop the use of still and motion cameras at football games, 1924 *NCAA Proceedings*, 70.

56. Howard Savage, *American College Athletics*, Carnegie Foundation for the Advancement of Teaching, Bulletin 23 (Boston: Merrymount Press, 1929).

57. Ibid., 224-65.

58. Ibid., 224.

59. Ibid., 240.

60. Ibid., 241.

61. J. R. Tunis, "Amateur Racket: Discussion of the Carnegie Report," *World's Work*, Dec. 1930, 52-54; "American School and College Athletics: Carnegie Foundation's Inquiry," *National Education Association*, Jan. 1930, 6; "Carnegie Lifts the Lid," *School and Society*, Jan. 13, 1931, 789.

62. See "College Athletics Much Improved Since 1929 Says Dr. Savage," *New York Times*, Nov. 7, 1930, 31; and "Reports Football Wanes in Colleges," June 15, 1931, 12.

63. "Decline in Revenue to Affect Sports Programs," *New York Times*, Jan. 4, 1931, sec. 11, 2.

64. 1933 *NCAA Proceedings*, 26.

65. Ibid., 28.

66. "Decline in Revenue to Affect Sports Programs," *New York Times*, Jan. 4, 1931, sec. 11, 2.

67. "Nation's Colleges Face Sport Crisis," *New York Times*, Jan. 15, 1933, sec. 3, 1.

68. 1931 *NCAA Proceedings*, 36.

69. "Does Radio Cut the Football Gate?" *Literary Digest*, July 16, 1932, 32.

70. This discussion is reported in *NCAA Proceedings* (Special Convention), July 29, 1932, 35-63.

71. An amendment removing this tax was attached to a bill that President Eisenhower signed on March 31, 1954.

72. 1935 *NCAA Proceedings*, 17.

73. Ibid., 109.

74. 1935 *NCAA Proceedings*, 90.

75. 1941 *NCAA Proceedings*, 142-45.

76. Ibid., 143.

CHAPTER 2

Controlling Competition and Enforcing the Rules

In the period between the end of World War II and 1960, the National Collegiate Athletic Association (NCAA) remained active in sports rulemaking and its various championship tournaments, but it began as well to take steps economists associate with the formation of a cartel. In this examination of NCAA activities affecting the input market—the interaction between the producers (athletic departments) and the employees (student-athletes)—we see the development and enforcement of a code restricting wages paid to student-athletes and a code restricting the methods of inducing an athlete to attend an institution (recruiting). The by-product theory of cartel organization serves nicely to put these NCAA actions into perspective.

THE BY-PRODUCT THEORY OF CARTEL ORGANIZATION

Cartel theory receives a good deal of attention in the standard economic literature.[1] Partly because of this inherent interest and partly because of the publicity the Organization of Petroleum Exporting Countries (OPEC) cartel received in the 1970s and early 1980s, most informed lay persons know that cartels restrict output in an effort to increase profits. One question that remains unanswered in all of this discussion, however, is how cartels are organized.

This inability to explain cartel formation has led readers to believe that a cartel is formed when all major producers in a particular industry coincidentally meet and suddenly begin to slice the market geographically and set production quotas. Or, in another version of the same belief, that a cartel is formed when selfish producers meet clandestinely and agree to limitations. Unfortunately, these scenarios, as well as most of the previous discussions of cartel theory, fail to explain how these meetings get organized. That is, standard cartel theory makes no mention of how the discussions or meetings that lead to market division and production quotas get started.[2]

Cost of organization is the economics term denoting the time and effort devoted to arranging meetings, carrying on discussions, and formulating a strategy. As related to cartel theory, cost of organization deserves consideration because it is one of the largest inhibitors of cartel information. In fact, the theory that follows postulates that once the cost of organization is overcome, it becomes relatively easy for a group to cartelize.

A cartel does not emerge, it evolves. It starts to take shape when a group of producers, who initially meet to discuss occupational or professional topics, begin comparing prices and production. They soon sense or learn that their competitive practices have left them all worse off than they would be in a less competitive market. Thus, one of the most important events in the sequence leading to the formation of a cartel is the establishment of a convenient association that invites producers to meet and exchange information.

Trade or professional associations make ideal places for industrial producers or members of an occupation to meet. These associations organize direct exchanges of information (through conferences and seminars) and indirect exchanges (through journals and newsletters) among members who are, nonetheless, competitors. Because of the ease with which information can circulate among competitors and because a majority of the industry—a necessary prerequisite for successful collective action—usually belongs, a trade or professional association makes the ideal place for spawning thoughts of collective action.

Trade or professional associations often form to solve a specific, recurring problem. Frequently, and especially in the professions, the solution to this problem is presented as a large benefit to the public. These groups undertake ventures portrayed as being in the public's interest, and the public, in response, suspends its skepticism, preferring to believe the association extraordinarily ethical or altruistic.

Over time, however, an association may begin to use its power to establish binding rules or regulations that limit membership opportunities or competitive practices. Advocated by members who may truly be altruistic or, more likely, by members alert to their true effects, rules that raise the cost of entry into the profession or restrict competition among members are developed. Regardless of their rationale, the rules that restrict entry or competition generally increase the wages of the members of the profession or decrease the quantity of the service supplied to the public relative to what one would expect in a competitive situation.

Economists call this behavior *the by-product theory of cartel organization* because industries and professions begin to cartelize as a by-product of their efforts to solve an industrywide problem. Most associations formed to solve a problem plaguing the entire industry realize that once they overcome the cost of organizing per se, the additional cost of establishing more restrictive rules is attractively low. These restrictions, broached along the way in public interest arguments, have the pleasant effect of providing those involved with increased financial rewards.[3]

Returning to intercollegiate athletics, we can see that the experience of the NCAA prior to World War II is totally consistent with the by-product theory. The NCAA was formed by a group of college athletic contest producers in response to an industry problem (widespread football violence and injury). The Association's early activities—organization of rules and championship events—were portrayed as in the public's interest. During this time the NCAA began conducting regular meetings (annual conventions) and other exchanges of information (published reports). Gradually, and simultaneously with its efforts to administer various intercollegiate sports, the NCAA started considering subjects other than rules and tournaments.

The by-product theory of cartel organization also asserts that a cartel forms from the experiments of a group attempting to maximize an objective function (for example, profit or industry efficiency). With this in mind, it can be shown that the cartelization of intercollegiate athletics evolved mainly from attempts of the games' producers to maximize athletic profits. To accomplish this, members of the NCAA used industrywide regulation to reduce the costs of staging the contests.

One of the most effective ways to cut costs was to reduce competition for student-athletes among schools; hence, out of NCAA efforts to control costs came restrictions on the inducements a school could offer an athlete. Furthermore, since the schools frequently violated these rules, the NCAA developed a strict method of enforcement to deal with cheaters. The remainder of this chapter follows the development of NCAA rules restricting competition between member schools and the establishment of an active enforcement mechanism.

THE SANITY CODE

On July 22, 1946, the NCAA called a Conference of Conferences in Chicago. At this two-day assembly, representatives from all the major athletic conferences met to discuss conditions in intercollegiate athletics. In addition to discussing the effects the end of the war would have on college athletics, the group considered efforts to force universities to obey the NCAA's rules, and the conference finally produced the first draft of a statement it called "Principles for the Conduct of Intercollegiate Athletics."

A copy of the five principles and a questionnaire went quickly to all members, and the response was so enthusiastic that at the 1947 annual convention, the membership adopted them as the guidelines to be followed when dealing with student-athletes. The NCAA went on to recommend that within the year all its members should be prepared to abide by the principles or lose their NCAA membership. Because it was believed that this code would return sanity to the process of recruiting and compensating student-athletes, the set of five principles became known as the Sanity Code.

Adoption of the Sanity Code was occasioned by many public assertions that it would preserve amateurism and protect college athletics. A closer look at the Sanity Code, especially section four, "Principles Governing Financial Aid to Athletes," reveals, however, that it was the NCAA's strongest effort to date to limit the cutthroat competition among its members for student-athletes. (Section four of "Principles" is set forth in Appendix C.)

Section four, the most important part of the Sanity Code, specifically detailed what financial aid an athlete could receive from a university. It stipulated that aid could be awarded only on the basis of need or scholarship (demonstrated in either high school or college), not solely on the basis of athletic ability. It also stipulated that the amount of aid could not exceed tuition and incidental fees. Many believed this section would ensure amateurism within college athletics, but whatever its effect in the ambiguous area of amateurism, the Sanity Code was a clear effort to limit competition for student-athletes.

If schools went unrestricted in what they would offer an athlete, they almost certainly would offer money. If all schools offered money, the talented athlete could conduct an auction for his services. The resulting increase in wages would obviously increase the cost of producing athletic contests. Therefore, efforts to limit payments to athletes also represented attempts to hold down athletic production costs.

Section four of the Sanity Code contained additional provisions to keep schools from bidding for athletes. The two most important codifications of the NCAA's postwar code stipulated that (1) all financial aid was to be administered by the office of financial aid, and (2) the student would receive a written statement of the exact amount of his award. These two conditions brought competition for athletes into the open and made nonsanctioned offers easier to detect.

The Sanity Code also included the NCAA's first attempt to punish violators. Any athlete who received unsanctioned aid would be ineligible to participate in intercollegiate sports, and, since the Sanity Code became part of the NCAA's constitution, a failure to adhere to its principles would (with the requisite two-thirds vote of the delegates to the annual convention) terminate that school's membership.

At the annual convention of 1948, the NCAA adopted the Sanity Code as the official set of rules for dealing with student-athletes. At the same time, the NCAA established a three-person Compliance Committee to ensure that the members actually followed the code. The first three members of the Compliance Committee included the chairman, Clarence P. Houston, athletic director at Tufts University; James H. Stewart of the Southwest Conference; and Ralph W. Aigler of the University of Michigan.

According to the NCAA constitution, the committee was

authorized to make rulings ... [and] to answer the inquiries as to whether stated practices ... are forbidden by, or are consistent with, the provisions of the Constitution. Such rulings and answers shall be deemed final and authoritative, subject to only reversal by a vote of the Association in convention assembled.[4]

The NCAA also set up a Fact-Finding Committee to conduct investigations whenever an inquiry was warranted.[5]

Even though the Sanity Code represented the NCAA's most thorough attempt in its 42-year history to enforce its rules, some parts of the code remained too vague to ensure the restrictions the NCAA sought. For example, one part of the new code allowed each school to determine the financial need of an athlete. The NCAA tried to persuade its members to evaluate an athlete's need the same as it would that of a nonathlete, but without specific instructions, financial need could easily vary from school to school.

It remained apparent that the Sanity Code would be difficult to enforce with only a three-person committee to oversee the compliance of

270 universities. But the Compliance Committee unexpectedly received help when some schools declared publicly that they would not abide by the Sanity Code. For example, on August 9, 1948, the University of Virginia called a news conference at its Charlottesville, Virginia, campus and announced that it would not adopt the code. Their spokesman said, "While we may agree with the spirit of the plan, it is the belief of our board that it cannot be enforced."[6]

Troubled by the University of Virginia's statement, the NCAA could do little at first because a school had to violate the Sanity Code before it could be prosecuted. In addition, the constitution guaranteed any school whose membership might be subject to termination four months' advance notification. The lack of an immediate reaction to Virginia's statement, therefore, represented not so much an unwillingness to deal with violators as a cumbersome enforcement process.

One year later, on July 27, 1949, the University of Virginia again rejected the Sanity Code, arguing this time that student-athletes at the school had to spend their spare time studying and could not, therefore, earn money to pay for items (such as room, board, and books) financial aid did not provide. Its acknowledged reputation for academic integrity, Virginia felt, entitled it to provide more aid to student-athletes than the Sanity Code allowed.

By mid-1949, the Compliance Committee had begun to find evidence of more violations than just Virginia's, and rumors circulated that the committee had the evidence to call for as many as 20 terminations at the next convention. In fact, one month before the 1950 convention, seven institutions were officially charged with violations: Boston College, the Citadel, the University of Maryland, the University of Virginia, Villanova University, Virginia Military Institute (VMI), and Virginia Polytechnic Institute (VPI).

The annual convention convened on January 13, 1950, and the Association moved quickly to consider the motion to terminate the seven memberships. The discussion of that motion revealed that shortly after its formation, the Compliance Committee had sent out a questionnaire to each active member of the Association, inquiring into the methods used to award aid. Having analyzed the answers, the committee sent out an additional 101 questionnaires. From these responses and from information provided by other sources, the committee authorized an investigation of 29 institutions. Conducted by paid investigators or by mailed inquiry, these investigations uncovered more than one incident at many institutions.

The Compliance Committee finally concluded that 20 institutions had violated the Sanity Code. It informed each school of its findings and gave them until July 1, 1949, to rectify the problems or at least to make clear in a letter that all violations would be corrected by September 1, 1949. Of the 20 institutions, 13 responded by July 1, detailing corrections they had or would make. These 13 were considered to be no longer in violation of the Sanity Code.

More letters were sent out to the seven remaining institutions in an attempt to commit them to the terms of the Sanity Code by September 1, 1949, but none responded satisfactorily. In accordance with the constitution, the Compliance Committee sent registered letters to the president of each institution informing him of the committee's intention to seek his school's ouster.

The NCAA's constitution mandated a certain procedure when a member faced termination. First, the school had to be notified of its predicament at least four months before the annual convention — this had been done in July 1949. Second, the Compliance Committee's resolution seeking the termination had to be approved by the Council and the Executive Committee. (Both bodies approved the termination resolution on January 12, 1950, the night before the annual meeting.) Third, the annual convention had to approve the termination resolution by a two-thirds vote. This last requirement was all that remained when the convention reconvened on January 14, 1950.

The motion calling for the termination of the seven memberships was placed before the convention by Compliance Committee Chairman Clarence P. Houston. He began the proceedings by briefly describing the violations alleged against each school. Each violation, not surprisingly, involved the award of excessive financial aid in all cases.

Charged with awarding excessive aid to football players, the University of Maryland had corresponded several times with the Compliance Committee but had never explicitly declared itself in conformity with the code. The Compliance Committee had written two letters informing Maryland's president of this lapse and asking him to be specific. The president wrote back to say he "presumed" the practice had stopped. But because he remained equivocal, Maryland was charged with a Sanity Code violation.

The Citadel, VMI, and VPI, military schools at the time, were all charged with awarding student-athletes excessive aid. The Sanity Code allowed a school to provide a student-athlete with only tuition and incidental fees, but military schools also provided room and board. The NCAA considered room and board more than incidental and charged the schools with violating the code.

Villanova, Virginia, and Boston College were also charged with providing excessive aid to student-athletes. Villanova admitted its violations in a series of letters to the Compliance Committee, but never answered the committee's last letter requesting more information.

Virginia had openly flaunted the extra aid it provided to student-athletes for more than a year. Boston College, which had been in violation during the Compliance Committee's investigation but had corrected the situation, was being prosecuted because it had technically been in violation during the investigation.

Representatives from each school addressed the convention, and most tried to persuade the membership not to vote for their termination. The delegate from the Citadel defended his school's financial policy by noting that a military college placed greater demands on a student-athlete's time than other schools. For example, because no Citadel student could leave the campus from 6:30 p.m. Sunday until 5:30 p.m. Friday, student-athletes could not defray their room and board expenses. The Citadel felt so strongly about its aid policy that it resolved to withdraw from the NCAA until it changed its rules to accommodate the Citadel's aid to student-athletes.

Representatives from the other military schools offered a similar defense. Walter S. Newman from VPI called it "impossible" for a student-athlete to earn enough money to purchase room and board, which was why the school remained in violation of the Sanity Code. William Coupers of VMI did believe, however, that conditions had changed at his school since September 1 and that it was no longer in violation.

The representatives of Boston College and the University of Virginia characterized the Sanity Code as an arbitrary mechanism that encouraged outside interference with internal college functions. The Boston College representative read a prepared statement noting that it could not "admit that a body set up for the handling of intercollegiate athletics can conceivably be more competent to judge a college's educational standards than the college itself."[7] Virginia felt its academic standards so demanding that it was impossible for student-athletes to hold part-time jobs, and it justified its aid policy as being in accordance, if only in spirit, with the Sanity Code.

Besides two members of the Compliance Committee, only one person spoke in favor of terminating the memberships. Victor O. Schmidt, Commissioner of the Pacific Coast Intercollegiate Athletic Conference (forerunner of the Pac 8, now Pac 10), noted that all members had agreed to the Sanity Code when it had been formulated two years earlier, fully aware of the punishment due a member who failed to comply. To Schmidt, retreating before actual violations seemed sadly ironic, and he colorfully summarized the choices for the voting membership: "Are we going to wear the red badge of courage [vote for termination] or are we going to show the white feather of surrender and despair [vote against termination]?"[8]

A secret ballot grouped the question of terminating all seven memberships into one motion, and the body voted 111 to 93 in favor of termination. But because the vote lacked the required two-thirds majority, the motion was defeated, and the first test of the Sanity Code enforcement mechanism failed.

The process that produced this failure revealed several flaws in both the Sanity Code and the NCAA procedures. The biggest problem with the Sanity Code was that it commanded only one effective form of punishment, membership termination. For any violations, flagrant or accidental, involving trivial or enormous amounts of unsanctioned aid, the Sanity Code subscribed one penalty.

In addition, the Compliance Committee procedures did little to encourage honesty. In many cases, the Compliance Committee received the information that led to investigations from the universities themselves. A truthful university with an ambiguous financial aid program risked its membership. A dishonest university that declared itself in compliance with the Sanity Code would undergo no further investigation. Under this de facto honor system, each school got a chance to decide whether to be honest or not.

The Compliance Committee's presentation before the annual convention of 1950 also highlighted organizational problems affecting Sanity Code enforcement. The time lag between the date the NCAA found a member in violation and the date it prosecuted the institution allowed a school to correct the problem before the case reached the Association. Membership termination was obviously inappropriate for Boston College, which had corrected its violations when it appeared before the 1950 convention, but it was charged anyhow.

Other problems included the fact that 1950 marked the first time the Compliance Committee had attempted to terminate a member's affiliation with the NCAA. Therefore, the seven cases precipitated considerable confusion when it came to matching the evidence with how the Association interpreted its Sanity Code. Did the appropriate university official respond to the inquiry? Did the university openly declare itself in compliance with the Sanity Code? What is the definition of an "incidental fee"? Does the Sanity Code adequately address regional or philosophical differences? All of these questions emerged at the 1950 convention, but no official answers followed — only an obvious need for still more detailed guidelines.

Finally, in its first attempt to terminate a school's membership, the NCAA revealed its inability to deal effectively with a large group. Both the Council and the Executive Committee, small groups, believed all seven schools guilty and deserving of removal. But once the issue was put before the large group, all sorts of extraprocedural maneuvering became possible: the formation of coalitions, vote trading, and so forth. Thus, if the NCAA was to develop a strict enforcement mechanism capable of effective punishment, this first experience suggested that it would be wiser to have smaller NCAA bodies deal with violators.

Second Thoughts About the Sanity Code

While the seven schools retained their memberships, they did not escape completely. Four days after the convention failed to pass the resolution to terminate, the Executive Committee declared each school a "member not in good standing," a sanction that banned them from NCAA meets or tournaments and was supposed to keep other NCAA members from competing with them. This sanction amounted to only a minor inconvenience, however, since the NCAA allowed scheduled contests to continue. (On February 25, 1950, the Council of the NCAA met and recertified Boston College a "member in good standing," consistent with the college's protests that it had corrected its violations before the 1950 annual convention.)

The Compliance Committee, meanwhile, continued its investigations. At the August meeting of the Council, Clarence P. Houston reported that the Committee had, in fact, investigated eleven institutions and that he had recommended six membership terminations. The *New York Times* reported the University of South Carolina and Clemson University to be among the six accused of violating the Sanity Code, and these two schools quickly threatened to leave the NCAA if it enforced the Sanity Code against them.

South Carolina and Clemson were not alone in wanting to limit the enforcement of the Sanity Code. Additional criticism came from a group of southern schools offering to propose amendments to curtail the activity of the Compliance Committee. But other schools, primarily from the North and specifically including the Big Ten Conference, publicly defended the code. As a result, the 1951 annual convention promised a clash between Sanity Code supporters, primarily small colleges and most northern schools, and its detractors, the large and southern schools.

Small colleges supported the Sanity Code because it placed severe restrictions on the financial aid a school could provide, thus conserving limited resources. Schools from the North, near most major cities and industries, also supported the code because it forced athletes to work for any aid beyond tuition and fees. These schools had an advantage because of the number of jobs available in their area. Generally, smaller colleges and northern schools supported the code because it helped keep down the cost of producing athletic contests.

Large schools wanted to change the code because they preferred to compete for athletes without restrictions. Similarly, southern schools, typically located in rural areas, realized that the code forced athletes to look for jobs in areas where job opportunities were scarce. In short, these schools favored changes that would enhance their recruiting advantages.

Not surprisingly, NCAA officials and members of the Compliance Committee supported the Sanity Code vigorously. The code, they argued, had been adopted at the request of those members disturbed by the growing number of rule violations, but now that the code was actually being enforced, some of the same members were complaining. Houston believed that the real problem was not the Sanity Code but an inclination by the schools to gain a competitive edge:

Do you think if we started out — well, let's say a foolish suggestion is that each and every athlete coming into that institution should be allowed a thousand dollars each year — that the alumni and the staffs of those institutions would be content?[9]

While the NCAA never officially embraced Houston's analysis, the smaller member schools apparently favored the Sanity Code because it helped equalize competition and allowed them a better chance of competing equally with the big-time schools. Other schools felt that the NCAA had no right to enforce the Sanity Code. They favored "institutional integrity," the prerogative to enforce Association rules themselves, back on campus. In fact, institutional integrity versus NCAA enforcement became an ideological point tied to the rights of a school to govern itself.

Lee Prater, athletic director at Northwestern State College in Louisiana, was typical of the proponents of local enforcement. He observed that, with few exceptions "every thing in my judgment, should be left to local conferences."[10] Almost certainly, some schools supported institutional integrity as a screen for their cheating, a point emphasized by James Lynah, Chairman of the NCAA Panel:

My experience . . . leads me to believe that [institutions] have been very loose and very derelict in the determination of need claimed by athletes to whom aid was granted.[11]

Among the five amendments designed to alter the Sanity Code introduced at the 1951 convention, the one that attracted the most discussion was Amendment D, which called for the deletion of section four of the Sanity Code, the section listing the restrictions on financial aid to student-athletes. The adoption of Amendment D would strip the code of all official limits on how much aid a school could offer a student-athlete and would, therefore, effectively neutralize the entire code. Some, including A. D. Kirwan, faculty representative from the University of Kentucky, argued for adoption on the grounds that one code simply could not address all the intercollegiate athletic problems in the country, and he presented the problem of providing aid for athletes in moralistic terms:

If it is not morally wrong to grant a student his institutional fees so that he may be able to go to college, and play football, why should it be evil to give him three meals a day and a bed to sleep in so that he may remain in college?[12]

The primary opponents of this amendment included, as we have seen, many small colleges, and S. W. Cram of the Central Inter-Collegiate Conference nicely synopsized their views:

We, of the small colleges, still need protection.... The structure and intelligence of a national group like the NCAA ... protects us from ... proselyting from larger schools. We are being confronted continuously by recruiting agents from the larger schools.[13]

Amendment D passed by more than the two-thirds majority, 130 to 60. When NCAA President Hugh G. Willet of the University of Southern California announced the tally, "there were cheers and much back-slapping."[14] The vote killed the Sanity Code, and returned NCAA rule enforcement to the individual schools, which, experience had proved, where disinclined to enforce them. It also allowed the Citadel to rejoin the Association and restored VMI, Virginia, Virginia Polytechnic Institute, Villanova, and Maryland to "good standing" status.

After the Sanity Code: Stricter Rules and Active Enforcement

The NCAA's experiment in code enforcement taught it several things. While the Association obviously needed an enforcement policy, the Sanity Code had clearly been too radical a departure from past policies and had introduced strict enforcement before the members were prepared for it. The NCAA would have to develop an enforcement policy much more gradually.

Accordingly, the next day, when the Association undertook major revisions in its constitution, it retained the Compliance Committee (by a 68 to 52 vote) even though it had no rules to enforce and no official purpose. Retaining the Compliance Committee proved a wise move, since it would later form the foundation of a much stronger enforcement committee than the one neutralized in early 1951.

The NCAA's 1951 convention also produced more constitutional changes than any other convention to that point. Parts of each section of the constitution were rewritten, and a major reorganization of the articles in the body and bylaws took place. The most significant of these revisions, as described by Victor O. Schmidt, Chairman of the Constitutional Revision Committee, was to transfer regulatory legislation and committee procedures to the bylaws, where they could in most cases be changed by a majority vote at any annual convention without notice.[15] The effect of requiring a simple majority vote to change or add a new regulatory section (instead of the previous policy of requiring a two-thirds vote) and the removal of the requirement that all members had to be notified in advance of the introduction of regulatory legislation lowered the cost of regulating and, in general, made it easier for the NCAA to control intercollegiate athletics.

In 1951, the NCAA Council took a more active role in establishing NCAA policy. In March of 1951, it established a subcommittee to help the Constitutional Revision Committee formulate regulations that would strengthen enforcement policies. At the Council's August meeting, the new subcommittee reported a 12-point program it had designed to eliminate many of the abuses in college sports. This 12-point plan included proposals to limit the number and amount of financial grants to athletes, to reduce undesirable recruiting activity, to demand strict adherence to the letter and spirit of NCAA rules, to penalize athletes receiving gifts or subsidies, and to eliminate excessive entertainment of recruits.[16]

The Council sent a copy of these recommendations to each NCAA member, elicited their opinions, and received responses indicating almost unqualified support. The Council interpreted the survey results as a mandate and began to formulate amendments to the constitution and bylaws to incorporate this 12-point plan. While the Council urged the membership to adopt these rules for a wide variety of reasons, most items in the 12-point plan served to limit competition for athletes. Thus, it seemed logical to expect that at the next annual convention, few schools would object to the adoption of regulatory measures that would lower production costs.

Among the more important changes made at the 1952 convention, the members voted 176 to 1 to replace the Compliance Committee with a nine-person Membership Committee empowered to

receive and consider complaints which . . . charge the failure of any member institution to maintain the academic or athletic standards required for membership. . . . The Committee shall have the authority . . . to institute an inquiry or an investigation. . . .

The Membership Committee may ... notify the Council that any member is ... subject to termination of its membership or other discipline. ... The Council shall thereupon determine whether it shall or shall not initiate proceedings for termination of membership or other discipline.[17]

At the urging of the Council, moreover, the convention adopted a measure to limit the aid student-athletes could receive, in direct accordance with the recommendations of the 12-point program. The proposed amendment was entitled "Principles Governing Financial Aid":

Any college athlete who receives financial assistance other than that administered by his institution shall not be eligible for intercollegiate competition; [excluding aid] received from anyone upon whom the athlete is naturally or legally dependent.[18]

Initially criticized as too lenient, the motion nevertheless passed 169 to 0.

While the 1952 convention attracted little outside attention, it addressed many important subjects. Equally important was the way in which, under the Council's guidance, it handled these issues. The Council had begun the year by studying conditions in intercollegiate athletics, developing a list of recommendations, and requesting the advice and guidance of the membership. With the approval of the members, the Council drafted several amendments and effectively portrayed them as the recommendations of the membership at large. The unanimity these resolutions attracted indicates how much better organized the leadership of the NCAA was during the 1952 convention than it had been at the previous two. Further testimony to the Council's adroitness is the fact that in 1952 the members overwhelmingly agreed to those measures designed to restrict behavior and enforce the Association's rules, measures that they had wrangled over and defeated the year before.

In 1952, the new Membership Committee began to function according to the rules outlined in the constitution. Shortly after investigating several schools, it found itself with insufficient resources to support its investigative work. To solve this problem, on April 18, 1952, the Membership Committee, with the approval of the Council, created a Subcommittee on Infractions. This subcommittee consisted of members of the Council appointed by the Membership Committee, and the NCAA's Executive Director, who served as chairman ex officio. The Subcommittee on Infractions was authorized to review all allegations of NCAA rule violations and investigate those it considered responsible. Having concluded an investigation, the Subcommittee on

Infractions was to issue a written report to the Membership Committee. The first Subcommitte on Infractions investigated numerous allegations but discovered no violations until it examined basketball at the University of Kentucky and Bradley University.

The University of Kentucky had won the NCAA basketball championship in the school year 1951-52, but in late April 1952, three of its players were convicted of gambling and point shaving in the 1949 season. Judge Saul S. Streit, who issued this verdict, had also jailed college basketball players the previous fall for similar offenses. At that time, Streit called college basketball a commercialized, professional venture plagued by fraud, forgery, and flagrant violations of amateur rules.[19]

At the 1952 verdict Streit called the athletic program at the University of Kentucky "the acme of commercialism and over emphasis" and was particularly critical of the school's basketball coach, Adolph Rupp, for associating with a known bookmaker.[20] Rupp responded by stating he would let Kentuckians be the judge of his actions, and the University issued a statement that claimed Streit's comments were "harsh and based on erroneous facts." But Streit countered by pointing out that "all facts stated by me were obtained from the lips of athletes, the coach, athletic director, and officials of the university."[21]

Comments by Streit during the trials received considerable attention, in part because members of the City College of New York basketball team were involved and the *New York Times* diligently reported on the trial. This attention put pressure on the NCAA to demonstrate that it was, in fact, in control of college athletics. The presence of behavior so obviously contradicting the standards that NCAA claimed it was upholding demanded that the NCAA effectively deal with these problems, especially in light of its Sanity Code failure. Consequently, in early May, NCAA President Hugh G. Willet vowed that the NCAA would investigate, and he directed the Membership Committee to look into basketball at Kentucky.

Accordingly, the Subcommittee on Infractions examined the Kentucky basketball program all the way back to the 1944-45 academic year. They found that players considered ineligible under NCAA rules had openly competed in NCAA events and found repeated violations of those NCAA statutes prohibiting payments to athletes. In short, evidence suggested a consistent pattern of flagrant rule violations by the athletic department at the University of Kentucky.

The University of Kentucky disciplined its own athletic program by limiting its grants-in-aid, restricting where the basketball team could play, restricting postseason tournament play, banning the team from Southeastern Conference competition for one year, and reprimanding

Adolph Rupp. These sanctions did not, however, deter the Council from recommending additional punishment, and the members of the Association subsequently approved these penalties:

1. [That] the University of Kentucky be placed upon probation for the academic year 1952-53;

2. [That] The Association direct the members of the Association to refrain from competing with the University of Kentucky in basketball during the academic year 1952-1953 [and]

3. [That] The Association declare that teams and athletes of the University of Kentucky are ineligible to compete in NCAA events during the academic year 1952-53.[22]

As a result of the harsh penalties instituted by the NCAA, Kentucky was forced to cancel its 1952-53 basketball schedule — a move that cost the University an estimated $125,000 to $150,000.[23]

Judge Saul S. Streit also sentenced three basketball players from Bradley University in the college basketball scandal, which led to an NCAA investigation of basketball at Bradley. The Subcommittee on Infractions uncovered evidence of both unauthorized payments and ineligible players, and even though Bradley, too, had enacted penalties against its athletic department, the Council recommended, and members of the NCAA approved, additional penalties similar to those imposed on Kentucky.[24]

In one very important way, the basketball scandal and the resulting trials and attention benefited the NCAA. Unable to penalize violators of its Sanity Code, the NCAA used the widespread outrage and public pressure for more penalties on the schools involved to sanction Kentucky and Bradley. Consequently, the NCAA emerged from the scandal as the generally recognized enforcer of amateurism in intercollegiate sports, a position it had been trying to attain since the end of World War II. The membership's approval of the NCAA's actions also showed them more willing to condone penalties less severe than membership termination. Moreover, knowing the types of penalties the members were likely to approve made it easier for the Council to gain support for its recommendations.

This experience also revealed to the NCAA's enforcers (the Membership Committee, the Subcommittee on Infractions, and the Council) how tedious it was to sanction a member. After investigating charges and deciding the penalties, the Council had to wait for the next convention before the sanctions could be approved and imposed. Citing this time delay and relying on its growing rapport with the membership, the Council proposed constitutional changes at the 1953 convention to streamline rule enforcement:

Disciplinary or corrective actions other than termination of membership or suspension may, on the recommendation of the Membership Committee, be effected during the period between annual Conventions by a two-thirds vote of the members of the Council present.[25]

Adoption of this proposal would allow the Council to issue all penalties short of suspension or termination between conventions without the full Association's approval.

Immediate criticism came from the southern schools, which had never liked the idea of outside enforcement and preferred the entire Association vote on sanctions. Most southern schools preferred voluntary enforcement, which allowed them greater freedom and fewer restrictions in recruiting and subsidizing student-athletes, a freedom threatened by swift enforcement. Voluntary compliance and a more methodical adjudication of violators spelled an advantage for the southern producers of intercollegiate athletic contests.

Typical of many who criticized the proposal, T. P. Head, athletic director at Louisiana State University, noted how the new rule resembled the old effort once tried and voted down. This proposal, he said, "appear[s] to be the old Sanity Code dressed up in a different suit."[26] Head was also shrewd enough to see that violators were penalized less severely when the entire membership could review the sanctions than when the Council acted alone.

Others argued that the NCAA badly needed a quick, efficient enforcement mechanism. Clarence P. Houston, Chairman of the Membership Committee and a member of the Council, pushed for passage of the proposal "so that it can be said with some sincerity that the NCAA is making at least an attempt to enforce the provisions of its Constitution."[27] The motion passed the annual convention 135 to 14, effectively increasing the enforcement power of the Council.

To increase the time available for investigations, the Council introduced a motion to push forward the date when a school had to be notified of its recommended termination. The constitution required that a school receive this notice by September 1, but the Council contended that this time constraint interfered with the investigations. Moving the date back to November 1 would make it easier to complete an investigation and still provide enough time for the school to prepare a defense. This proposal passed without debate.

During the year, the Membership Committee inquired into 35 alleged violations. By the end of 1953, it had dismissed 9 cases and reported 6 cases to the Council for action, but 20 cases remained to be investigated. This backup led the Council once again to review its procedures. The main problem, it concluded, lay in the many redundant steps the investigative procedure required. First, the Subcommittee on Infractions had to investigate and report to the Membership Committee, which then had to report to the Council. Since all the members of the Membership Committee and most members of the Subcommittee on Infractions also belonged to the Council, the same case was being reported twice to essentially the same group. A simple solution would be the elimination of the Membership Committee.

At the 1954 convention, the Council proposed dissolving the Membership Committee and upgrading the Subcommittee on Infractions to a full committee. The Committee on Infractions would retain its three members, but it would enjoy all the powers of the Membership Committee. In one of the shortest parliamentary maneuvers at any NCAA convention, the motion passed unanimously without any debate or discussion.

(Later, in 1958, the Council adopted additional rules to make enforcement still more efficient. As the rules stood in 1957, once the Council imposed sanctions, the school could appeal to the Council, which often required the Council to hear the same case twice. To eliminate this duplication, the Council ruled that

When a penalty has been imposed by the Council . . . there shall be no review of the penalty by the Council except upon a showing of newly discovered evidence . . . or that there was a prejudicial error in the procedure which was followed.[28]

With the enactment of this ruling, the only appeal open to a school without new evidence was to the entire Association at the annual convention.)

Other steps at the 1954 convention taken to strengthen the enforcement mechanism included the approval of the Council's plan to force all schools to certify their compliance with NCAA regulations. This "Certification of Compliance" required the chief executive officer at each university to certify in writing that his school was breaking no NCAA rules in its dealings with student-athletes. The plan went into effect on May 7, 1954.

In 1954, the Council took punitive action against many more schools than ever before. Among its most widely publicized penalties were those imposed on the City College of New York, the University of Miami (Florida), and the University of Portland. City College received one-year probation on October 20, 1954, for "paying" athletes to play basketball and forging transcripts to use ineligible players. Transporting athletes home at Christmas break got Miami one-year probation and prevented them from participating in any NCAA tournaments during the 1954-55 academic year. Portland was only reprimanded when its newly appointed coach held out-of-season tryouts for positions on the basketball team. In all, Frank N. Gardener of Drake University, Chairman of the Committee on Infractions, reported that "of the 53 cases, 39 have been completed. Of the 39 completed cases, the Committee reported violations of varying degrees in 14. These were subsequently acted upon by the Council of the Association."[29]

RESTRICTING COMPETITION FOR AND PAYMENTS TO STUDENT-ATHLETES

Between late 1954 and the annual convention of 1961 the NCAA enacted many rules restricting the behavior of those who produced intercollegiate athletic contests. Prominent among these were restrictions on the methods of recruiting athletes and limits on the compensation paid to a participant in college sports. While all these rules purported to preserve amateurism, they also limited economic competition among schools and controlled the cost of producing athletic contests.

In 1954, the Council adopted rules that limited the monetary competition for student-athletes by restricting the financial aid a school could offer. According to the Council's minutes,

the Council considered two [proposals that] would limit athletic aid . . . and, also, place a ceiling on the amount of unearned financial aid an athlete might receive from all sources.

It was the sense of the meeting (unanimous show of hands) that the Council issue an interpretation limiting aid to an athlete's undergraduate period.[30]

In a similar effort, the Council began to study the practice of recruiting athletes, and it established a special committee to examine the role of booster groups and the excessive transportation of prospects.[31]

Because financial aid and recruiting costs had to be borne by the producers of athletic contests, the limits on payments to student-athletes and restrictions on recruiting behavior amounted to cost-cutting measures. Moreover, since these restrictions and limits allowed schools to compete on a more equal footing for the services of student-athletes, they also helped ensure more even competition between schools.

The NCAA began early to dictate how a school could recruit a student-athlete. At the 1950 annual convention, for example, it had established this bylaw on recruiting:

No member of an athletic staff or other official representative of athletic interests shall solicit the attendance at his institution of any prospective student with the offer of financial aid. . . .

No members institution shall . . . pay the traveling expenses of any prospective student visiting its campus, nor shall it arrange for or permit excessive entertainment of such prospective student during his visit there.[32]

Clearly, rules like this served to restrict competition among NCAA schools; however, the Council's desire in 1954 to reexamine the recruiting process indicates that even these earlier rules were inadequate to prevent member schools from competing for athletes.

The special Committee on Recruiting appointed in late 1954 reported to the Association in 1956. It had found schools spending huge sums to recruit student-athletes, lavishing on them all-expenses-paid trips to campus, gifts, and imaginative entertainment. Furthermore, when such separate groups as the alumni associations or the booster clubs wanted to beguile and entertain prospective student-athletes, the universities often had no control over what were essentially recruiting activities.

Student-athlete recruitment had intensified in the 1950s. Because the jet airplane made it easy to travel widely, a coach could now search nationwide for talent. As a result, the best athletes found themselves wooed by many more schools, often dozens or even hundreds of them. Lynn O. Waldorf, football coach at the University of California, described recruiting in the mid-1950s this way:

[I]t is not at all unusual for a boy who weighs 190 pounds and can run 100 yards in ten seconds with a football under his arm, to . . . visit six or eight campuses three or four times in some cases, one or two times in others. It is a wonder to me that a boy in his senior year is able to keep up with his studies to the point where he can graduate.

In cases where home visitation is permitted . . . a boy will be visited by 10 or 20 different coaches a great many different times.[33]

Other members of the NCAA echoed this desire to reduce the disruption in a student's last high school year. But while all the NCAA professed concern for the high school athlete, few believed it to be the real reason the Association sought to limit recruiting. A more plausible explanation would be, once again, the desire to reduce the cost of the product.

To neutralize the effect of one school's recruiting blandishments, another school would visit an athlete and bring him to campus several times. As interest in the prospect intensified, other schools then had to visit and entertain the athlete. In the process, all the schools increased their recruiting expenditures. If, however, the schools would agree to limit the visits and the entertaining, no one school's recruiting position would change and all would lower their costs.

The NCAA also wanted to curtail recruiting for yet another reason: It had no reliable way to tell what happened to an athlete during his recruitment. Having limited financial aid to athletes, the NCAA increased the temptation to arrange for secret payments, gifts, and entertainment. Because the inherently secretive process of recruiting gave schools another chance to engage in pecuniary competition for a prized recruit, the NCAA sought to control recruiting in order to curtail this competition and save the schools money.

The Committee on Recruiting drew up strict restrictions that limited the length of an athlete's campus visit and the money devoted to his entertainment. Informal surveying revealed that few members favored these strict limitations. As a result, Earl S. Fullbrook of the University of Nebraska, Chairman of the Committee on Recruiting, introduced at the 1956 convention these "more liberal" proposals that were adapted from his committee's earlier report:

No member institution shall finance more than one visit to its campus for any prospective student-athlete....

No member institution shall . . . finance the transportation costs incurred by relatives or friends of a prospective student-athlete.

No member institution shall arrange for or permit excessive entertainment of any prospective student-athlete.

No member institution shall permit an outside organization or agency to utilize or administer funds for the purpose of transporting prospective student-athletes to its campus.[34]

Considerable opposition to Fullbrook's proposals arose at the 1956 convention. Many considered national control on recruiting impractical; better, they said, that the individual athletic conferences make and enforce such rules. These opponents introduced their own recruiting legislation known at the time as "The Dartmouth Amendment":

No member of an athletic staff or other official representative of athletic interests shall solicit the attendance at his institution of any prospective student with the offer of financial aid....

No member institution shall . . . pay the traveling expense of any prospective student visiting its campus.[35]

The Dartmouth Amendment received its name because the idea of completely banning recruiting by the university athletic staff had been introduced and championed in the early 1950s during the Sanity Code fight by representatives of Dartmouth College. By this time, however, Dartmouth was no longer an active proponent of the amendment, even though the college name continued to be associated with the notion of no athletic recruiting.

The Dartmouth Amendment superficially resembled the Fullbrook proposals, but a close reading reveals that no limitations were placed on such nonuniversity groups as alumni associations and boosters. For precisely this reason, the NCAA leadership strongly opposed it. Members of the Committee on Recruiting argued that the looseness of the Dartmouth Amendment, and particularly its failure to limit visits funded by outsiders, would spur rather than reduce recruiting. Worse, those members unable to finance recruiting visits or entertainment might actively solicit help from outside groups. This sort of outside assistance had already led to ambiguously allocated transportation funds, and the constant fear was that once an alumni association became deeply involved in recruiting, it would be difficult for the school to control its activities. This problem troubled the NCAA because it had devised no way to control alumni associations either. As Frank N. Gardener of Drake University observed,

I can assure you that the Committee on Infractions has found it extremely difficult to ascertain all that goes on between that alumnus and that boy to prevail on him to attend that institution even on a visit.[36]

When the time came to consider recruiting rule changes, the more recent Dartmouth Amendment appeared on the agenda first and won acceptance. But the membership also agreed to authorize an additional study of recruiting practices, and a motion that the Council submit definite recommendations at the 1957 convention also passed.

At the 1957 convention the Council reported the results of its yearlong study and confirmed what the Committee on Recruitment had already observed—that the members were spending preposterous amounts of money to lure athletes. The Council concluded, as the Committee on Recruiting had earlier concluded, that unchecked competition between schools should be avoided.

The Council introduced a constitutional amendment designed to prevent this destructively competitive recruitment by limiting, in general, what a school spent on a recruited athlete and by preventing alumni associations and booster groups from recruiting athletes behind the university's back. The amendment specifically limited recruiting visits to two days and two nights, forbade schools from transporting relatives of a recruit and from entertaining the prospect excessively. Importantly, the proposed amendment made it clear that the institution was solely responsible for administration of the recruiting funds:

All funds for the recruiting of prospective student-athletes shall be deposited with the member institution. The institution shall be exclusively and entirely responsible for the manner in which it expends the funds.[37]

Solidly backed by the Council, this proposal, unlike the earlier proposal from the Committee on Recruiting, occasioned little debate and passed easily.

During 1957, the NCAA Council also addressed once again the amount of financial aid a member could award to student-athletes. In the mid-1950s the Council had begun to issue "official interpretations" of its rules and to publish them in a special section of the constitution. By adding more interpretations each year, the Council had built an elaborate system of working definitions for the concept of "an amateur." Only after the interpretations had become complex and lengthy did the Council officially begin to specify what compensation an amateur student-athlete could accept.

Before 1957, the Council allowed a school to pay only a student-athlete's "commonly accepted educational expenses." But without a more specific definition, the NCAA encountered problems when schools, in good faith or not, stretched this definition to include automobiles, airplane tickets home, suits of clothing, and restaurant dining. In mid-1956 the Council decided to clarify its vague definition of aid and ruled that "commonly accepted educational expenses" included "tuition and fees, room and board, books and . . . $15 a month laundry money."[38]

This ruling constituted the first specific limit on what an NCAA member could provide a student-athlete. It simplified investigations for the Committee on Infractions, which no longer had to debate whether a payment to an athlete was justified. And since schools often used educational "stipends" as inducements, the ruling also constituted the NCAA's strongest move yet to limit competition for athletes.

In the late 1950s, intercollegiate athletics began to attract the sort of media attention that focused more on athletic administration than on the traditional area of athletic performance. Athletic recruiting continued to dominate these stories. As schools competed vigorously to attract better athletes, a study conducted by the Big Ten Conference reported that athletes were actively comparison shopping among schools. In one case a father was reported to have arranged a coast-to-coast vacation trip for himself and his son, free on the basis of an itinerary that took them on expense paid visits from campus to campus.[39]

The most publicized scandal in college athletics during this time involved the Pacific Coast Conference, which, in August 1956, sanctioned four of its schools for oversubsidizing its athletes. UCLA received three years' probation, USC and Washington were placed on probation for two years, and California got one year's probation. All were prohibited from having their games televised and from participating in the postseason Rose Bowl, which had a contractual agreement to pit the conference champion against the Big Ten champ every New Year's Day.

New conference rules were instituted that limited athletes to earning $100 a month (in addition to room, board and tuition provided under scholarship) at a $2-an-hour job. Rules were also instituted to limit the number of grants-in-aid a school could provide to 150, but the effectiveness of this limitation was suspect because no ceiling was set on the grants-in-aid that could be established with outside contributions. In the middle of this controversy Victor O. Schmidt, conference commissioner, resigned his $16,800-a-year position to practice law.

At one point USC and UCLA decided to quit the conference, but eventually the problems resulting from having a conference composed of schools with major athletic programs (USC and UCLA played their home football games at Los Angeles Coliseum with a seating capacity of 101,528) and schools with less ambitious programs (Oregon, Oregon State, Idaho, and Washington had stadiums seating less than 30,000 each) were resolved. USC, however, was put on probation in 1959 by the NCAA for the second time in four years for violations similar to those that got it in trouble in 1956. Its penalty included two years without a television appearance, a move that cost them an estimated $100,000.

In 1959, the presidents of two Ivy League schools took widely reported swipes at intercollegiate athletics. A. Whitney Griswold of Yale called the athletic scholarship "one of the greatest swindles ever perpetuated on college youth." He went on: "Its aim is not the education of the youth, but the entertainment of its elders, not the welfare of the athlete, but the pleasure of the spectator."[40] Asked about Griswold's remarks, Princeton University President Robert F. Goheen agreed: "Institutions have gotten so deeply into the entertainment business that they have gotten away from the proper realm of amateurism."[41]

As the decade came to a close, the NCAA instituted several minor constitutional changes that helped in subtle ways to limit recruiting competition by ensuring that the recruiting process remained open and observable. For example, in order to monitor payments to student-athletes, the NCAA amended its rules at the 1959 convention to include this restriction, which made it much easier for the Committee on Infractions to determine the amount of financial aid a student-athlete received:

In all cases, the institutional agency making the award of aid shall give the recipient a written statement of the amount, duration, conditions, and terms thereof.[42]

Not all efforts to restrict competitive recruiting practices originated within the Council of the NCAA. In 1959 the possibility of introducing a national letter of intent once again was voiced at the annual convention. This effort had begun in the early 1950s when discussions about recruiting practices revealed that some athletic conferences had already tried to prevent wasteful competition for student-athletes. Delegates from the Southwestern Conference described an ingenious innovation they had borrowed from the Southeastern Conference called the letter of intent, which was

a printed agreement . . . which in reality states that this prospective athlete agrees to enroll at the said institution, and within this document it states what he shall receive as far as financial aid is concerned. . . . There is no penalty if the boy does not enroll in the institution, but if that boy signed a letter of intent with one of our Conference institutions, he is ineligible if he decides to enroll in any other institution.[43]

The Southwestern Conference had adopted the letter of intent in 1952, and most considered it a good idea. Said Madison Bell of Southern Methodist University, "When a boy once signs the letter the other schools leave him alone and he doesn't have to worry about recruiters at his doorstep."[44] While Bell emphasized the advantages to a high school boy of arresting the recruiting process after the April 1 deadline, the schools obviously liked the letter of intent because it saved them the money they might spend trying to keep other conference schools from "stealing" their recruits. It also saved them the money they might spend trying to steal someone else's recruit.

While no official action on the letter of intent was taken in the mid-1950s, it reappeared in the general roundtable discussion at the 1959 convention. The roundtable seminars at each convention provided the forum where several speakers presented short talks on sports-related subjects and then entertained questions and comments. By 1959, four distinct roundtables were held at each convention: the athletic director's roundtable, the faculty representatives' roundtable, the general roundtable, and the college roundtable. The subject matter ranged widely at these discussions, but at the 1959 general roundtable it focused sharply on the idea of a national letter of intent applicable to all NCAA members and would supersede limits in a conference letter of intent.

During the discussion, most of the representatives wondered why a superior high school athlete would want to commit himself when any school would enroll him at any time, or what would happen if any athlete changed his mind after signing a national letter of intent. Representatives of the Southwest, Big Ten, Southeastern, and East Coast

Conferences detailed for the group the letter of intent policy their respective conferences followed.[45] These descriptions, natural complements to the general discussions, nevertheless pictured the letter of intent as an attractive way to limit recruiting competition between schools already competitors in the intercollegiate athletic industry.

The by-product theory of cartel organization introduced earlier holds that when producers meet, it is natural for them to discuss ways to limit competition. Standard economic theory teaches that these discussions often appear during attempts to form a cartel. In light of these tendencies, it is clear that the 1959 general roundtable constituted a key exchange of information between producers consciously attempting to limit competition for materiel. The meeting and discussion of production techniques by the producers of intercollegiate athletic contests with this specific intent to limit competition was identical to the actions one would expect from producers in any industry seeking to restrict competition.

NOTES

1. See the discussion in James M. Henderson and Richard E. Quandt, *Microeconomic Theory: A Mathematical Approach* (New York: McGraw-Hill, 1980), 175-90; and Roger LeRoy Miller, *Intermediate Microeconomics: Theory, Issues, and Application* (New York: McGraw-Hill, 1978), 305-11.

2. Nowhere in George W. Stocking and Myron W. Watkins, *Cartels in Action* (New York: Twentieth Century Fund, 1946), a lengthy book about many of the cartels that have existed in the United States and the international arena, is there a discussion of how the cartels were organized.

3. Mancur Olson presents another by-product theory for collective action by certain groups in *The Logic of Collective Action* (Cambridge, Mass.: Harvard University Press, 1965).

4. *Proceedings of the National Collegiate Athletic Association*, 1948, 222 (hereafter cited as *NCAA Proceedings*).

5. Ibid., 195-96.

6. "Purity Code Rejected," *New York Times*, August 10, 1948, 28.

7. 1950 *NCAA Proceedings*, 202.

8. Ibid., 205.

9. 1951 *NCAA Proceedings*, 154.

10. Ibid., 168.

11. Ibid., 155.

12. Both quotes come from 1951 *NCAA Proceedings*, 209.

13. Ibid., 211.

14. "NCAA Drops Sanity Code Control of Financial Aid to Athletes," *New York Times*, January 13, 1951, 19.

15. Ibid., 215.

16. 1952 *NCAA Proceedings*, 106.

17. Ibid., 262-63.

18. Ibid., 254.

19. "Scallazzo is Jailed with Five Players in Basketball Fix," *New York Times*, November 20, 1951, 26.

20. "Judge in Fix Case Condemns Kentucky Teams and Coach," *New York Times*, April 30, 1952, 1.

21. Both comments are from "Two Plead Guilty in Basketball Fix," *New York Times*, May 8, 1952, 27.

22. 1953 *NCAA Proceedings*, 269-70.

23. "Kentucky to Keep Coach Rupp Despite Basketball Disclosure," *New York Times*, November 5, 1952, 37.

24. See 1953 *NCAA Proceedings*, 273 for the exact penalties.

25. Ibid., 313.

26. Ibid., 257.

27. Ibid., 260.

28. 1958 *NCAA Proceedings*, 234.

29. 1955 *NCAA Proceedings*, 267.

30. Ibid., 134.

31. Ibid., 264.

32. Ibid., 352.

33. 1956 *NCAA Proceedings*, 161.

34. Ibid., 196.

35. Ibid.

36. Ibid., 190.

37. 1957 *NCAA Proceedings*, 299.

38. Ibid.

39. "College Football - Has It Really Gone Pro?" *U.S. News and World Report*, Oct. 26, 1956, 57-58.

40. "Yale Head Finds Swindle in Athletic Scholarship," *New York Times*, February 24, 1959, 1.

41. "Goheen Supports Griswold's Stand," *New York Times*, February 25, 1959, 67.

42. 1959 *NCAA Proceedings*, 249.

43. 1956 *NCAA Proceedings*, 165-66.

44. Ibid., 166.

45. See 1959 *NCAA Proceedings*, 192-202.

CHAPTER 3

Controlling Television and Postseason Bowl Games, 1945-60

Toward the middle of the twentieth century, changes in technology made it possible to broadcast college football on an exciting new medium—television—that enabled many who had never been to a college game to experience the excitement of a Saturday afternoon gridiron clash. But television also invited fans who otherwise would have gone to the stadium to stay home and watch a remarkably satisfactory substitute for the real thing. Athletic directors and college administrators, concerned with the revenue football generated, saw television as a mixed blessing.

In addition to television, college officials were also concerned about the number of games played after the regular football season concluded. Since the end of World War II, postseason bowl competition had expanded rapidly, with football games springing up in warm, and not so warm, climates to exploit regional loyalties. During this period, however, sponsors of these games were not connected with the NCAA, and there was general concern about how the proceeds from the bowls were divided.

In this period these two problems, closely associated with the rapidly growing interest in college football, began to concern the National

Collegiate Athletic Association (NCAA) acutely. How the NCAA dealt with the increasing ubiquity of television and the proliferation of football bowls provides the focus for this discussion.

THE NCAA AND TELEVISION

The Effect of Television on Attendance: the NORC Study

The first televised college football game was played on September 30, 1939, at Randalls Island, New York City, between Fordham University and Waynesburg College. Fordham won 34-7 in a game that was broadcast locally by station WXBS.[1] However, television attracted little attention at the time, with only a few stations and a few thousands sets in the entire country.

After World War II, the television industry and its appetite for sports coverage grew quickly, prompting the NCAA to speculate on the effect it would have on college athletics. The two most important questions the NCAA set about to answer were (1) how television broadcasting of college games would affect attendance and gate receipts, and (2) how the NCAA might exploit television.

A preliminary attempt to appraise the effect of television occurred at a roundtable session during the NCAA's 1948 convention. The main speakers at the roundtable included representatives from several television stations, from Northwestern University, which had begun televising its football games in 1945, and from the Don Spencer Company, a promotional group trying to obtain exclusive rights to sell college sporting events to television. During this discussion different opinions about the effect of television broadcasting on college sports, and particularly on football, surfaced.

Some believed that television would increase interest in football. Those who shared this view equated television in 1948 with the early days of radio when an outcry arose against football broadcasts. Radio, it was noted, had produced no detrimental effects on attendance; in fact, it had helped increase attendance by building interest in the game.

Some supported television sports as a service to those unable to reach the stadium. For example, Bill Durney, assistant to the president of St. Louis University, noted that during the 1947 season a group of 20 elderly priests had been able to watch the Billikens play on television. Without television, he argued, football would not be accessible to shut-ins and others who could not come to the stadium.[2]

Others arguments made to support the televising of college sports included the notion that it would provide a school with increased publicity. As Harold P. See went on to assert, "Complete television coverage of college sports will provide publicity for the institution, which in the future will have no parallel." See also argued that television could be used to keep alumni affiliated with the school's endeavors: 💲 donations

Clever use of the medium by educational institutions may easily serve to bring forth contributions and donations to the sport budget from graduates who might have lost some interest.[3]

Ted Payseur, athletic director at Northwestern University, urged members to pursue television with caution, noting that Phil Wrigley, the owner of the Chicago Cubs, had advised him, "We don't know a thing about television, and what is more, neither do the television people."[4] Payseur also pointed out that while in 1947 only 19 television stations were actually broadcasting, 54 had received licenses and 64 more applications were pending, so that in a year's time 137 stations could be broadcasting. Furthermore, in the previous year, the number of television sets had increased from 8,000 to 170,000 and might increase fivefold in the next year. Because of the changes taking place in the industry, Payseur recommended that members avoid long-term television commitments by making their television plans a year at a time.

Don Spencer, of the Don Spencer Company, petitioned the NCAA to let his company promote all of the NCAA's television productions. Spencer took a businesslike approach to the problems associated with televising college sports, and he addressed himself directly to the most important issue: how television would affect attendance and gate receipts. Noting that television provided free admissions, he recommended the appointment of a national NCAA television control committee and a national representative to handle the sale of television rights.[5]

Spencer strongly believed that together, an NCAA television committee and a national representative (his company) could reduce or eliminate many of the problems caused by televising college games. The coordinator and representative could determine which area of the country would view what games and how to divide the money from the broadcasts, the rebroadcasts, and the highlight shows. In short, Spencer envisioned an organization "for the regulation and coordination of network sports programs emanating from colleges." Its primary functions would be to standardize rates on a sound national basis, assuring a fair return to all schools, and to eliminate the bargaining of one school against the other by advertising groups in their attempts to purchase television rights.[6]

While no official position was endorsed at the meeting, the 1948 roundtable discussion illuminated the major problems and interests involved in televising college sports events. Spokesmen for the television industry cited promoting fan interest or providing a public service as reasons for televising college games, and naturally they deemphasized the possibility that television would erode attendance. The owners of television stations, who cared little for gate receipts but stood to gain from broadcasts, favored the unlimited televising of college games. On the other hand, promoters like Don Spencer saw the chance to profit by ensuring that colleges maximized their football dollars, and he recommended policies designed to regulate the sale of broadcast rights and administer sports productions once they reached television.

At the end of its 1948 convention, the NCAA membership was divided on the question of the effect of televising college sports events. Those who equated the television problem with the advent of radio 20 years earlier and, therefore, believed that television would promote attendance, could point to no empirical confirmatory evidence. Furthermore, these people tended to ignore the fact that the television experience came closer than radio to the actual experience, and others who argued that this high degree of "substitutability" would logically decrease attendance had a good case. Suddenly, the NCAA had become acutely aware of the problems television could present, and it had few solutions. As is often the case, it was decided a study should be conducted, and the NCAA appropriated $5,000 for an independent agency to determine the exact effect of television broadcasting on college sports.

At the 1949 convention, the results of this study were made public. Conducted by Crossley, Incorporated, of New York, the study was little more than an opinion survey about television, and it had followed questionable techniques. Nonetheless, the study did suggest some trends:

Football attendance dropped from 1946 to 1947; also from 1947 to 1948—though not enough to be alarming.

In 1948 television did not ... create an interest that translated into ticket purchases.

Fifty percent of set owners rate television as good or better than attendance, which is an alarming figure considering the rapid increase of the production and purchase of television sets.[7]

At the same time this survey was being conducted, the Eastern Collegiate Athletic Conference (ECAC) began to examine the evidence used to argue that television broadcasting would stimulate fan interest. The television industry had frequently cited professional baseball as a sport that had televised its games without suffering a decline in attendance. College authorities dissected this argument and found that major league attendance had increased with television, but attendance in the minor leagues had fallen.[8] Television broadcasters did point out that they would pay for the college football broadcast rights, inferring that the payments could offset any lost attendance. Ironically, however, college officials believed that there was no prospect of getting any kind of a figure that would be commensurate with the possible loss of revenue.[9]

Given these results, and supported by the NCAA's study, the ECAC reasoned that television would have a great, if not fatal, effect upon small schools and schools located in small centers of population. Therefore, it concluded that television would definitely result in decreased revenues, that television contracts should be made on a one-year basis only, and that no contract should be made in 1949.[10]

Other universities had found that televising games seemed to have no effect on attendance. Prominent among these schools was Notre Dame, whose representative, the Reverend John H. Murphy, pointed out that

We do not know from one year to the next whether it is a good thing or a bad thing to televise our games. We have not noticed any attendance drop off in the two years we have had our home games televised, and all of the home games in the two years have been televised.[11]

Murphy's remarks were prefaced, however, by NCAA Secretary Kenneth L. Wilson, who noted that Notre Dame's broadcasts had such strong appeal that television had recently spent around $100,000 to pipe its games into the Chicago area.[12]

Partly because of the lack of facts and partly because of the division on the issue in the membership, the NCAA took no action on television at the 1949 convention. Instead the Association decided to spend more money studying the problem. Nonetheless, the discussion at the 1949 convention presaged the differences in the membership that were certain to emerge once the NCAA undertook to adopt a television policy binding on everyone.

If it were true that television decreased attendance at small college games, the smaller schools could be counted on to support a policy that restricted television broadcasts. Conversely, those larger schools with attractive football programs that had already sold their broadcast rights and experienced no decrease at the gate would hardly favor such an agreement. Thus, virtually any television policy the NCAA tried to adopt would surely arouse opposition.

The 1950 convention included a roundtable presentation by Jerry N. Jordan, a graduate student in psychology at the University of Pennsylvania, who had studied the effect of television on attendance at college football games. His work, begun while an undergraduate at Princeton the previous year, was titled "The Effect of Television on Living Habits." It had been generally well received and won him membership in Sigma Xi, an honorary society, for original research.[13]

Jordan's study suggested that if television exerted any effect at all, it was to increase attendance, though in areas heavily saturated by television, attendance increased less than in areas with less home viewing. Jordan had conducted his study around Philadelphia, with many television sets and 15 football college teams. Accordingly, he concluded that "the fear that televising of a big college [game] would hurt a small college [game] does not seem to be substantiated."[14]

This study flatly contradicted the findings at the previous convention, but the members found reasons to doubt Jordan's work. Jordan's study focused on the behavior of those individuals living within a 50-mile radius of Philadelphia, and he made no attempt to adjust for a population density large enough to mask attendance fluctuations at college games. Without adjusting for population density and the nearly insatiable appetite for sports in the Philadelphia area, it was impossible to believe that Jordan's study represented anything more than a record of the behavior of the citizens of the Philadelphia area, not a theory applicable to the entire United States.

Interestingly, Jordan conducted his study at the University of Pennsylvania, which had been broadcasting its football games for almost ten years and was destined to become one of the leading opponents of NCAA-regulated television. Whether any connection existed between Penn's desire to avoid NCAA involvement and the results of Jordan's work, one cannot say, but the University of Pennsylvania assisted and supported his research and would doggedly continue to cite the study well into the 1950s, when the NCAA undertook to regulate the televising of college sports.

At the same convention, Ralph Furey, athletic director at Columbia University, presented results of the television survey the ECAC had conducted in lieu of an NCAA survey that remained incomplete. The ECAC, with more experience in television and more Association members (38) than any other conference, had sent out 30,000 questionnaires and analyzed 12,000 responses. It based its report to the 1950 convention on a preliminary inspection of 2,300 responses picked at random.

These responses suggested that 27.1 percent of the alumni of large colleges believed that watching a game on television was better than actually attending a football game, while 38.3 percent of the alumni of small colleges believed this. Accordingly, the ECAC reasoned that smaller schools would be more greatly affected by televised college sports than larger schools. Based on its study of television, the ECAC recommended

the immediate appointment of an active and representative television commit-tee of the NCAA [to] ... make a thorough investigation of all material now available and report to the Executive Committee of the NCAA. ...

Pending any possible action at the 1951 convention, we urge the NCAA recommend to its members that no television commitments be made beyond the 1950-51 college year.[15]

Tom Hamilton, athletic director at the University of Pittsburgh, supported this motion because of what he had observed while a member of the football staff at the Naval Academy:

As television sets grew in numbers in the area, our attendance figures went down, and from a monetary standpoint ... the remuneration that came in from television only amounted to about 300 seats at the stadium, and we felt that probably thousands stayed away.[16]

Schools in the Midwest expressed a willingness to support more study on the effect of television, but they resisted legislation to control it. Ted Payseur of Northwestern, who conducted a survey of schools in the Midwest, made these observations:

[The University of] Wisconsin figures it [television broadcasting] did not affect their season ticket sales. ... Ohio State, for instance, has only one year of television. It has not affected them whatsoever. ... At Northwestern, we televised for four years. I would say definitely it does not have an effect on our season tickets.[17]

Nonetheless, when the ECAC's motion was put to the entire Asso-ciation, it carried a voice vote, and a committee was appointed to study television. It received instructions to report the next year, during which time all members were advised to avoid long-term television commitments.

The 1951 convention began with the reports of the vice-presidents of the eight districts, and a strong theme on the harmful effect television had on football attendance quickly appeared. Lloyd P. Jordan of Harvard reported that his district had experienced a decrease in foot-ball attendance and "on the basis of careful analysis it would seem that live television is the cause for this attendance decline."[18] H. P. Evert of the University of Washington summed the feelings of most when he reported, "The inescapable conclusion is that television wounds beyond the point of endurance."[19]

Because many attributed a decline in attendance to television broadcasting, the NCAA's control over television became the central issue at the 1951 meeting. At the large College and University Group roundtables, representatives from many schools offered opinions about what should be done. The ECAC called for a moratorium on live football broadcasts and wanted the NCAA to experiment with delayed televising and different forms of cable television in an effort to determine how each affected attendance.

Herbert O. "Fritz" Crisler of the University of Michigan revealed that the schools in the Big Ten had already met to discuss television, and they had decided to ban live television in the 1951 football season. Crisler was a strong supporter of the NCAA's attempts to control broadcasts. At the previous convention, to counter the public service argument cited to support unrestricted broadcasting, Crisler pointed out:

I appreciate the public service aspect. However, I don't believe our stadium full of good will and public service on five or six afternoons in the fall will help us a bit on our budget.[20]

Both Crisler and Wilbur Johns of the Pacific Coast Conference shared the experience of their respective conferences, experience that indicated television had caused both attendance and revenue to tumble. They concluded that colleges ought to attempt to impose some form of control on television broadcasting.

To settle the question of television's effect on attendance once and for all, the NCAA had authorized the National Opinion Research Center (NORC) to study the subject. Their survey, delivered to the 1951 convention, carried more credibility than any of the previous studies because it relied heavily on attendance and television broadcasting statistics. The preliminary results of the NORC study solidly supported the hypothesis that television produced a decrease in attendance.

The survey used the 1947 and 1948 attendance averages to adjust for home-and-home series arrangements between schools with stadiums of different sizes.[21] The survey showed that in 1949 football attendance at all games jumped 3.3 percent over the 1947-48 average and that in 1950 football attendance at all schools declined .3 percent compared with the 1947-48 average. But overall attendance in 1950, when there was more television broadcasting than the previous year, dropped 3.5 percent from 1949. Furthermore, when the survey divided schools according to areas receiving televised games and areas not receiving televised games, the statistics became more convincing. Between 1949 and 1950, attendance at football games fell 6 percent in areas with access to televised games, while in areas without televised games, attendance increased 2.5 percent. (Table 1 shows these trends.)

The NORC study also adjusted for team performance to see how on-field success affected attendance. While the findings supported the idea that the superior teams (those winning 75 percent or more of their games) would continue to draw even with television, the results also

Table 1
Attendance Trends for Colleges in TV Areas and Outside Them

	Percent Change From 1947-48 Average		Percent Change 1949 to 1950
	1949	1950	
All Colleges	+ 3.3	- 0.3	- 3.5
Colleges in TV Areas	+ 1.9	- 4.2	- 6.0
Colleges Outside TV Areas	+ 6.6	+ 9.3	+ 2.5
District 1 - New England	+ 2.6	-24.4	-26.3
In TV Areas	+ 0.7	-28.2	-28.7
Outside TV Areas	+12.1	+ 1.1	- 9.8
District 2 - East	- 5.8	-19.5	-15.5
In TV Areas	- 8.1	-23.0	-16.2
Outside TV Areas	+21.3	+33.3	+ 9.9
District 3 - Southeast	+ 4.7	+ 4.6	- 0.1
In TV Areas	+ 2.5	+ 1.6	- 0.9
Outside TV Areas	+ 7.4	+ 7.9	+ 0.5
District 4 - Midwest	+ 0.6	+ 1.0	+ 0.4
In TV Areas	+ 0.2	- 0.1	- 0.3
Outside TV Areas	+ 1.7	+ 4.1	+ 2.4
District 5 - West Central	+12.2	+11.4	- 0.7
In TV Areas	+11.1	+11.6	+ 0.5
Outside TV Areas	+13.8	+11.1	- 2.4
District 6 - Southwest	+16.0	+34.0	+15.5
In TV Areas	+26.9	+49.7	+18.0
Outside TV Areas	+ 4.9	+20.5	+14.9
District 7 - Mountain	+13.4	-10.2	-20.8
In TV Areas	+14.5	-18.7	-29.0
Outside TV Areas	+12.8	- 6.1	-16.8
District 8 - Pacific	+ 0.3	- 3.4	- 3.7
In TV Areas	+ 0.6	- 5.8	- 6.4
Outside TV Areas	- 1.5	+ 8.1	+11.0

Source: 1951 *NCAA Proceedings*, p. 147.

adversely

Table 2
Attendance in Relation to Team Performance

	Percent Change in 1950 Attendance From 1947-48 Average	
Colleges with Teams which won	IN TV Areas	OUTSIDE TV Areas
75% or more of games	+ 9.8	+12.6
50-74% of games	- 2.9	+13.8
25-49% of games	-23.1	+ 2.5
0-24% of games	-22.7	- 1.5

Source: 1951 *NCAA Proceedings*, p. 147.

suggested that television broadcasting dramatically reduced attendance at games involving below average teams (those winning between 25 and 49 percent of the time) and inferior teams (those winning between 0 and 24 percent of the time). To highlight the magnitude of these effects, the survey showed that all but the inferior teams that played outside the range of television experienced attendance increases during the study period. (Table 2 presents the figures on attendance related to performance.)

As Table 3 shows, the NORC conclusion—that television adversely affected game attendance—also held true in regions experiencing different levels of television penetration. But the evidence that gave the NCAA greatest pause was the record (shown in Table 4) of the absolute number of people who attended games in 1950. This part of the study repeated the initial results: that overall attendance in 1950 had dropped slightly from the 1947-48 average and that this drop included both a 4.2 percent decrease in areas offering televised games and a 9.3 percent increase in areas without televised games. The 4.2 percent decrease represented nearly half a million fans who stayed home from the games, and the NCAA delegates, who typically included the athletic director or football coach, understood the implications in falling gate receipts. The NORC also divided its statistics into regions to show which geographic areas gained (the Southwest) and lost (the East) with unrestricted television broadcasting. (These figures appear in Table 5.)

After hearing the results of the NORC study, the NCAA's Television Committee presented its recommendations: Institute a system to

Table 3
Attendance in Relation to Number of TV Sets in Area

Percent of Families owning TV Sets	Percent Change in 1950 Attendance From 1947-48 Average
50-59% (8 areas, 35 colleges)	-18.3
40-49% (11 areas, 29 colleges)	- 4.2
30-39% (9 areas, 15 colleges)	0.0
20-29% (14 areas, 28 colleges)	- 5.5
1-19% (13 areas, 21 colleges)	+11.1
Areas without television	+ 9.3
Colleges in areas where 30% or more of families own TV sets	-10.1
All other colleges	+10.7

Source: 1951 *NCAA Proceedings*, p. 148.

control television, and provide members with appropriate payment for
the rights to their games. The committee also recommended a moratorium on live college football telecasting, and it proposed a Television

Table 4
1950 Attendance in Major and Minor Colleges

	1950 Actual Attendance	1947-48 Average Attendance	Percent Change
Major Colleges	13,261,446	13,253,430	+ 0.1
Minor Colleges	1,399,861	1,457,226	- 3.9
Total	14,661,307	14,710,656	- 0.3
In TV Areas			
Major Colleges	9,190,244	9,569,118	- 4.0
Minor Colleges	838,275	903,549	- 7.2
Total	10,028,519	10,472,667	-4.2
Outside TV Areas			
Major Colleges	4,071,202	3,684,312	+10.5
Minor Colleges	561,586	553,677	+ 1.4
Total	4,632,788	4,237,989	+ 9.3

Source: 1951 *NCAA Proceedings*, p. 148.

Table 5
Attendance in Major Conferences

Conference	1950 Actual Attendance	1947-48 Average Attendance	Percent Change
Big Seven	974,775	790,982	+23
Big Ten	2,223,408	2,175,504	+ 2
Ivy League	1,120,025	1,498,252	-25
Mountain	366,494	429,425	-15
Pacific Coast	1,557,956	1,670,990	- 7
Southeast	1,765,922	1,784,342	- 1
Southern	865,331	791,058	+ 9
Southwest	1,221,891	879,479	+39

Source: 1951 *NCAA Proceedings*, p. 148.

Committee with representation from the eight districts. The Television Committee would establish an NCAA policy on the use of filmed highlights and on television programs about college football while encouraging the use of such pay television features as cable (phonevision and skiatron) and theater television.

Accepted at the preliminary roundtable, the Television Committee's recommendations became a motion to be presented in the business portion of the annual convention. Throughout these maneuvers, however, persistent opposition came from the Universities of Pennsylvania and Notre Dame, each of which was already earning substantial revenues televising its games.

Francis Murray, athletic director at the University of Pennsylvania, spoke against the Television Committee's recommendations. He argued that, despite the NORC study, insufficient facts existed to warrant the measures. Murray reported that the University of Pennsylvania had been televising its football games for a decade, yet attendance had fallen only in 1950, a decrease he attributed to the bad weather in the fall of 1950 more than to television. He also questioned the legality of the agreement, and he reemphasized the public service provided by a policy of unlimited football broadcasts.

Notre Dame's faculty representative (who later would become the school's president), the Reverend T. M. Hesburgh, was also against the moratorium. He asserted that a binding NCAA plan would hurt Notre Dame because the publicity from television attracted many of the quality students that made Notre Dame "a better school." He also invoked the public interest argument:

[W]e must always think of the public because it is the public that supports our sports program, and the more of them that knows our program, that follows our program, the wider support we should get.[22]

But few members sided with Notre Dame and Penn, and most believed they would benefit under a policy of NCAA-controlled television. In a 161 to 7 vote, the Association passed the recommendation of the Television Committee, which stated:

[T]he members of the NCAA agree to declare a moratorium on live telecasting of college football games for 1951, and ... a committee consisting of one member from each NCAA District [should] be appointed by the Executive Committee to work on and direct this project of the NCAA.[23]

Hindsight reveals that this resolution gave the NCAA more power to limit competition between the producers in the intercollegiate athletic industry than it had ever before enjoyed in its 45-year history. Before the NCAA television policy, each school had been free to maximize its football profits by selling television broadcasting rights and charging admission fees. But television's increasing technical capabilities had begun to place many, often far-flung, schools in direct competition for the spectator's entertainment dollar. With television, a fan had the choice of attending a local game or staying home to watch nationally known teams. As the NORC study indicated, fans were attracted to televised football, which eroded attendance in all areas served by television.

One can find in basic economic theory an explanation for the NCAA's problems with and responses to television in the late 1940s and early 1950s. In any competitive industry, producers try to maximize their product's profits. As all producers expand production, however, the profits of the group decrease toward zero. This is precisely what had begun to happen in college football. As schools sought to earn as much money as possible from their games, they found themselves competing with each other through television, and it was believed that this competition decreased the earnings for more schools than not.

One possible solution to this dilemma is for all firms in the industry to organize to restrict industry output and increase the product's price. By dividing the marketplace or setting quotas and establishing a mechanism to ensure compliance, the resulting cartel raises profits. This is exactly what the NCAA chose to do.

(Whether or not television broadcasting was responsible for the decrease in attendance is an interesting question to modern observers, but it seemed not to trouble NCAA members at the time. They saw attendance falling concurrently with an increase in the televising of college games and did not particularly care if anything more than a strong correlation between the two events existed. As a rationale for collective action, the appearance of this relationship was just as important as a detailed understanding of cause and effect. While the NORC study was not the most rigorous piece of work, it provided the NCAA with the evidence it needed to justify collusive behavior.)

The moratorium on live television and the NCAA's subsequent plan to restrict its use obviously limited competition among schools. Deprived of television broadcasts, more fans could be expected to attend college games. In addition, it could be expected that the price of broadcasting rights for those few games the NCAA allowed to be shown would rise. Thus, the NCAA response to television equates to the division of the marketplace and a limit on competition that is part of cartel theory.

One can further interpret the establishment of a Television Committee to organize and supervise the NCAA's television policy as the method by which the production quotas would be arranged and enforced. The Television Committee had the power to select which games would be televised and where they would be shown or, in other words, to ensure that all producers followed the agreement. To penalize members who might ignore the NCAA's television policy, the Council recommended that any such school be declared a "member not in good standing." By a mail vote, more than two-thirds of the members approved this idea, along with the Council's proposal to recommend the expulsion of any member who flouted the television resolution.

The NCAA's First Binding Television Plan

The nine-member Television Committee met frequently after the 1951 convention to discuss the problem of television broadcasting, and after consulting many authorities in the field, it adopted a plan to control the number of games broadcast, the areas in which those broadcasts would be shown, and the division of the revenue. In this plan, one game would be shown on seven of the ten Saturday afternoons from late September to late November, with blackouts scheduled for three Saturdays. A team could be televised twice (at home and away), and the proceeds from the sale of the television rights would be divided, with 40 percent to the two schools involved and 60 percent to the NCAA for research and promotion. Throughout the season NORC was to continue its study of attendance trends.[24]

Most of the objections to this plan came from members who considered it too lenient. Only the Universities of Pennsylvania and Notre

Dame objected that it exercised too much control over a member's television appearances. They also objected to the proposed 40-60 revenue split, arguing that the Television Committee had no constitutional authority to exact this sort of payment and that a school should be free to make its own financial arrangements. While both Penn and Notre Dame argued from self-interest—the NCAA would cost them the money they were earning on previously negotiated contracts—other schools agreed that the 40-60 split ought to be put to the vote of the entire Association. Consequently, the Television Committee retreated, later dropped the 40-60 revenue division, and substituted a plan to assess a fee (a percentage of the broadcast payments) on those schools whose games were broadcast in order to finance future television research.

Even after this change, the University of Pennsylvania remained in conflict with the NCAA policy and vowed to continue broadcasting all its home games. In response, the Council declared Penn a member not in good standing, and immediately four other Ivy League schools—Cornell, Columbia, Dartmouth, and Princeton—informed the University of Pennsylvania that they would not play their 1951 games with the Quakers.

The University of Pennsylvania believed the NCAA to be in violation of antitrust laws and appealed for help to the Federal Department of Justice. But the Justice Department was, ironically, fully occupied with an antitrust case against the National Football League (NFL) owners for colluding to negotiate the league's television contract, and they could spare no time for the University of Pennsylvania. At this point, Penn reconsidered its decision and agreed to abide by the NCAA's television policy.

The initial announcement of the NCAA's television policy rasied uncertainty and distress in the business community. The television networks and sponsors deferred negotiations with the NCAA, hoping it would be unable to act collectively. Television manufacturers opposed the plan because they believed it would reduce the public's interest in television. But when the University of Pennsylvania failed to carry out its own broadcasting plan and all of the approximately 300 NCAA members agreed to follow the new television policy, sponsors quickly lined up to petition the NCAA for television rights.

In contrast to the modern televising of college football games, in which only the major networks bid for the broadcast rights, both television and corporate sponsors bid for and won the first NCAA football television rights. No doubt this was because television networks were so small in 1951 that the automobile, oil, or appliance sponsoring companies could negotiate with the many small stations interested in broadcasting games just as easily as the networks.[25] In any event, the NCAA awarded the rights to the Westinghouse Electric Company because of its willingness to participate in a public relations program and its "offer of 2.5 times the station rate as a minimum payment to the competing institutions was one of the two equally high bids."[26]

The Westinghouse Electric Company chose the National Broadcasting Company (NBC) to broadcast games, but other independent stations also carried them. In 1951, television broadcast 20 games in which 30 different college teams appeared. Through the NORC, the NCAA carefully monitored these broadcasts and estimated that some 35 million people had seen all or parts of a televised NCAA football game in 1951.

The broadcasting itself went very nearly according to plan. One game was broadcast in all areas of the United States on seven weeks of the ten-week season, and each area was blacked out on three Saturdays. Because the network could not set up a broadcast by the first Saturday (September 22, 1951), this date counted as one of the three blackouts in all areas. Westinghouse and the NORC chose the other two blackout dates in each area.

The NCAA's 1951 television plan featured the first color broadcast and the first coast-to-coast broadcast of a college game. The color telecast took place on September 29, 1951, when the Columbia Broadcasting System (CBS) featured the 35-0 whitewash of the University of Pennsylvania by the Golden Bears of the University of California from Franklin Field in Philadelphia. The coast-to-coast broadcast occurred when 36 stations of the NBC system showed the October 6, 1951, 14-10 home victory of the Illini of the University of Illinois over the Wisconsin Badgers.[27]

While the television plan required adherence to strict rules, the NCAA relaxed some of these rules just enough to gain important public goodwill. Rather than arbitrarily enforcing its blackouts, the Television Committee's plan occasionally permitted broadcasts of games considered to be in the public interest. A good example of this occurred on October 20, 1951, in the game between Virginia Military Institute and Duke University. Originally the game had not been scheduled for television, but since all proceeds were earmarked for the Shrine Crippled Children's Fund and (perhaps more important) because the game was sold out, the Television Committee agreed to televise it. This decision not only created goodwill with the Shrine Foundation, but it also provided the NCAA with evidence of its own flexibility and public service. In addition, because the game was sold out, these valuable benefits had come cheaply.

The NCAA also remained aware of the special relationship it enjoyed with the federal government. While legal questions may have hovered over the NCAA's collective television policy, the federal government appeared unwilling to investigate it. The NCAA, in turn, avoided any behavior that might reverse this benign neglect. In particular, it made special provisions in its 1951 broadcast season to accommodate those government officials who were also football fans in and around Washington, D. C., and who possessed the power to curtail the NCAA's television policy.

For example, the NCAA made special arrangements for the Washington, D. C., area to view the game between Notre Dame and Michigan State at a time when the area had been scheduled for a blackout. To accommodate the Washington fans, the NCAA pushed the area's blackout date back until November 17, 1951, and showed the November 10 Notre Dame-Michigan State game.[28]

The NCAA publicly rationalized the change by claiming "there was no game available for fans to attend on that date," even though the United States Naval Academy was playing against the University of Maryland in Baltimore, Maryland, some 30 miles from the center of Washington.[29] The far more plausible explanation, obviously, was the NCAA's desire to please those Washington football fans with the power to investigate its competition-reducing television policy. Indeed, it is no coincidence that the NCAA dropped its scheduled blackout the day after *Washington Post* sportswriter Shirley Povich, in the lead article in the sports section, called for the Federal Department of Justice to investigate the NCAA television policy.[30]

While the NCAA's television plan could be flexible when it meant generating goodwill among Shriners and Congressmen, the NCAA also proved early that it would not bow to grassroots pressure. On November 24, 1951, the television plan called for the third blackout of the southeastern United States. On that day, however, the University of Kentucky had scheduled the University of Tennessee. Louisville television station WHAS and the Louisville *Courier Journal* mounted a campaign to televise the game, because it carried immense local interest and was sold out. When Westinghouse, the NORC, and the Television Committee decided to maintain the blackout, WHAS and the *Courier Journal* continued applying pressure, going as far as to contact the Department of Justice (which did nothing). They ceased only when the University of Kentucky, which did not support the effort, sent the Television Committee a telegraph stating it would not televise the game under any circumstance.

The television station and the newspaper insisted that their campaign had served the best interest of the public: they had only wanted all the fans to enjoy the game. What they failed to mention was that they both stood to gain monetarily from a televised Kentucky-Tennessee game since they had recently invested in new electronic equipment to accommodate it.[31] Their extraordinarily vigorous attempts to get the game televised—arousing the public and contacting the Justice Department—suggest that college football broadcast revenues in 1951 were already substantial.

The NCAA, meanwhile, defended the Kentucky blackout by claiming that the accuracy of its $50,000 television research program would be seriously jeopardized if the game were shown. This may have been true, but it is also possible that the NCAA wanted to prove itself immune to pressure from even the most rabid football fans. If it had given in to the Kentuckians, it would have had difficulty resisting similar campaigns in the future. More important, the NCAA television policy promised across-the-board profits only if the NCAA continually resisted the inevitable pressure to show blacked-out games. In this case the NCAA's response to pressure from WHAS and the Louisville *Courier Journal* was logical because, unlike the broadcasting of the Shrine benefit game or the Notre Dame-Michigan State game, which were also sold out, the Association had relatively little to gain (Louisville goodwill paled before Congressional goodwill) and much to lose (the erosion of the policy and the profits it promised to yield).

In addition to television broadcasting, however, the NCAA was also conducting experiments with theater television, color television, cable television, and the sale of postgame film.[32] The NCAA discovered that theater television generated large sums of money in blacked-out areas, and by the end of the 1951 season, it could supply seats for 200,000 viewers (at admission fees as high as $2.40 per seat) in theaters associated with the program. The NCAA postponed its experiments with color television because of the Defense Department demands during the Korean War, and its cable television efforts proceeded slowly because of the general lack of appreciation in the 1950s for its potential.

NCAA Television Plans, 1952–60

Despite its restrictive television broadcasting policy, however, attendance at all NCAA college games again fell, this time by 6 percent in 1951.[33] While this fall could be attributed to events besides television (the records of the teams involved, changes in personal disposable income, the weather, and so forth) the Television Committee noted with some optimism that attendance in television areas had fallen only 4 percent, compared with 6 percent the year before.

Both the Television Committee and the NORC admitted that their study was too limited to be conclusive. Consequently, the Television Committee urged that the study continue and that the membership adopt a 1952 television policy similar to the one used in 1951. Specifically, the Television Committee recommended an NCAA controlled and directed television plan for the 1952 football season designed to "minimize the adverse effects of live television upon attendance at college and high school football games [and]... to spread television among as many colleges as possible."[34] The Television Committee was directed to draw up a plan and have the membership vote by mail referendum, and the members were instructed not to enter a television contract or agreement until a plan was approved.

Representatives of most NCAA schools favored the resolution, but Francis Murray, athletic director of the University of Pennsylvania, who believed his school to have suffered large financial losses under the policy, once again spoke out against it, citing it as a bad example of commercialism in collegiate sports.[35] Murray went on to argue that the television policy was inconsistent with the NCAA's constitutionally stated policy of institutional control of athletics, but he failed to convince more than seven others, and the members ultimately adopted the second NCAA television policy, 163 to 8.

A closer look at the University of Pennsylvania's position reveals some of the problems economic theorists predict for a cartel. Whenever a group of producers colludes to form decisions collectively, one of the first problems to emerge centers on income distribution. If the opinions of all the members receive equal weight (for example, each member has one vote and a simple majority rules), a redistribution of income from the wealthier members to the poorer members will occur. This redistribution may, however, threaten the cartel's survival because the specter of this redistribution provides the wealthier producers with an incentive to withdraw, assuming the penalty for withdrawing is not greater still.

The strenuous objections of the University of Pennsylvania (and, from time to time, of Notre Dame, as well) are consistent with what we know of individual behavior in collusive groups. Without the NCAA's limitations, Pennsylvania and Notre Dame attracted generous television contracts. With the NCAA limitations, the Pennsylvania and Notre Dame revenues were, in effect, redistributed to those other schools that appeared on the NCAA's weekly telecast. Furthermore, under the NCAA's decision-making rule, the two schools could do little about it. Because a majority of NCAA schools stood to gain from the television policy, Penn and Notre Dame found themselves constantly outvoted on questions of television policy.

Notre Dame suffered perhaps the greatest loss of any school under the NCAA's television policy during this period. It estimated the value of its lost television appearances at $600,000 in 1951 and $1 million in 1952. As Moose Krause, athletic director at Notre Dame, remarked, "The NCAA started as an advisory body, then became a regulatory body and now has become a confiscatory one."[36] Nevertheless, neither Notre Dame nor the University of Pennsylvania withdrew from the Association, because Penn's experience the year before, when its rival schools threatened a boycott, demonstrated that without competition from the NCAA members, neither could fill a football schedule.

During the 1952 football season, the NCAA's television policy permitted football telecasts on 11 Saturdays featuring 11 national games and 12 small college games involving a total of 46 teams. In addition, under the NCAA's sell-out rule, 10 more games were shown for a grand total of 33 games and 51 different teams. These 51 schools divided $1,151,109.22, less than a 12 percent assessment to cover the NCAA's expenses.[37] This money was divided among the 51 schools by a formula based on the number of stations that carried a particular game. Thus, the schools that received the largest payments were the U.S. military and naval academies, whose annual Army-Navy game was carried nationwide.

Under the NCAA's 1952 television policy, overall attendance at college football games fell 1.1 percent.[38] But the most interesting statistic revealed that while paid attendance in 1952 was about the same as in 1951, attendance at colleges facing TV competition remained 16 percent below their average pretelevision 1947-48 base, while colleges which were not exposed to television competition drew 10 percent larger audiences than they did in 1947-48.[39] While the Television Committee had no way to determine what would have happened to attendance with unlimited broadcasting, it speculated that "with unlimited telecasting at present saturation levels, one can only assume that attendance in TV areas, which will soon include the whole country, would again turn sharply downward."[40]

In 1953, the NCAA again employed NORC to study the effect of television on attendance, but to ensure that NORC conducted the study properly, the NCAA also hired Benson and Benson, a market-research organization, to evaluate the NORC effort. Benson and Benson ratified the NORC work, pointing out that their research found that restrictions on televising college football lessened its negative impact on attendance.[41] Based on declining attendance and the reports of the two independent research agencies, the Television Committee recommended that the members again adopt a television plan similar to those used in the previous two football seasons.

Once again, the Universities of Pennsylvania and Notre Dame objected vigorously to the committee's annual television policy. Penn's Francis Murray launched a lengthy attack on the results of the NORC study, noting that even with controlled broadcasting, attendance at ten of the smaller schools in the Philadelphia area had declined, a result he attributed to forces unrelated to television. Notre Dame drew up a list of ten reasons why the Television Committee should not control college television broadcasting and distributed its list to all convention delegates and the press.[42] As it had in 1951, Notre Dame couched its appeal in altruistic terms. Representing Notre Dame, President Theodore M. Hesburgh noted:

We believe that the current plans of restricted television have not been in the public interest. On the contrary, they have attempted to dictate what the public can and cannot see with little regard for what the public would like to see.[43]

Despite the best persuasive rhetoric of Notre Dame and Penn, the membership voted 172 to 13 to accept the Television Committee's general resolution and agreed to vote by mail on its specific provisions. On April 25, 1953, the Television Committee sent each school a copy of its specific television plan, and by May 4, 1953, the plan passed 157 to 12. NBC, which had bid for the television rights in association with General Motors, received the contract.

Under the television plan in effect during the 1953 football season, the NCAA arranged for one broadcast on each of 13 dates (12 Saturdays and Thanksgiving). In an effort, moreover, to ensure more teams a television appearance, the policy allowed a college only one televised game a season (the one-appearance rule), and it stipulated that at least one game during the year be shown from each of the eight geographical districts. The plan also allowed sold-out games to be shown, and under this agreement, 11 other games reached home screens. Only three of these sell-outs, however, were shown in addition to rather than instead of the originally scheduled game. Under other provisions of its 1953 policy the NCAA also conducted experiments with panorama presentations and cable television.

A panorama presentation consisted of showing parts of four football games during the time one game would normally be played. Television crews set up in Princeton, New Jersey; Memphis, Tennessee; Champaign, Illinois; and Iowa City, Iowa, transmitting during the afternoon parts of the games being played there. While the crews experienced no technical difficulties switching from city to city, the fans who watched the presentation thought it disjointed, and over 90 percent of those fans who contacted General Motors the next day disliked it.[44] Consequently, the October 24, 1953, presentation marked the NCAA's first and last attempt to combine four live broadcasts into one show.

By contrast, pay-as-you-go television met with much success. The initial reports of several experiments with cable television indicated that fans were willing to pay to see televised games. The NCAA found three types of cable systems capable of transmitting without difficulty: phonevision (a telephone hookup with a charge), skiatron (involving a ticket inserted in a slot), and telemeter (a coin-operated arrangement). In late 1953, however, the Federal Communications Commission had not yet approved any of these systems.

By 1953, a college appearing on a televised game could expect to earn substantial revenue. Payments ranged from the $25,000 for each of the participants in the four games televised during the panorama presentations (that is, $200,000 divided by the eight participating teams) to the $123,930 divided (according to whatever agreement they struck) between the two schools that appeared in one game televised by 92 different stations. The average payment for the 11 single-game telecasts that season was $120,306 divided between the two participants.[45]

Even with the NCAA's ongoing policy of strict television control, college football attendance in 1953 fell by 3.51 percent.[46] This further decline led the Television Committee to recommend once more that it prepare a policy for the 1954 season similar to the plan it used in 1953. The Television Committee issued a recommendation to the 1954 annual convention advocating a mail vote for a television policy to be developed later and urging all schools to refrain from television commitments for the 1954 football season. The recommendation was adopted 172 to 9 and the 1954 plan was approved by the membership through the mail.

The television policy the Committee developed for the fall of 1954 called for one broadcast each Saturday, one apprearance for each school, and at least one broadcast originating from each of the eight geographical districts. With this policy in effect, college football attendance increased 2.2 percent in 1954, the first increase since the NCAA instituted its television policy.[47] Armed now with positive results, the Television Committee recommended that a television plan similar to the 1954 plan be employed in 1955.

Because the specific television policy never took shape until midyear, the Television Committee had been continually asking the annual convention to approve a general resolution calling for the committee to study and recommend a television policy to be voted on during the year. But at the 1955 annual convention, in addition to the general resolution of the Television Committee, six separate and specific television plans were offered by the membership at the convention. The new proposals called for more regional broadcasting and reflected the increasing popularity of broadcasting sporting events throughout a delimited area.

The move to develop a television policy that provided for regional broadcasts stemmed from the successful experience of the National Football League (NFL), which had been showing six games a weekend within the geographical area of their origin. The NFL's regional television policy appeared to be more popular than the NCAA's practice of showing one national game in all areas of the country, and the idea of college football adopting a more regional orientation received strong support from conferences located in sparsely populated states.

Conferences such as the Big Ten (in the Midwest) and the Pacific Coast Conference (on the West Coast), whose fans were located in large areas and whose teams had few schools in the area to compete with, supported the regional plan. Schools in the Big Ten felt so strongly about the regional plan that they threatened to withdraw from the NCAA if the 1955 television plan was a copy of the 1954 plan. (It was generally believed that the Big Ten was quite serious and that if it left, the Pacific Conference would follow, jeopardizing the NCAA.) Schools in the East, located closer to each other than most other schools, opposed the regional plan backed by the Big Ten because it would increase competition for exposure. Numerous small colleges from the Midwest also spoke out against the plan because of the harm Big Ten broadcasts would inflict in terms of decreased attendance.

When it came time to decide which television policy to adopt, the membership had three different options. First, the NCAA's Television Committee called for the readoption of the policy employed in 1954. Second, a few schools supported a return to unlimited broadcasting. Third, many schools expressed interest in one of the four national-regional plans, which would divide the country into several television regions and allow a school to broadcast one football game a year in the region. A straw vote revealed an overall preference for a compromise regional plan (introduced by the ECAC) over a national plan (very similar to the previous year) 84 to 81, but parliamentary procedure dictated that the only resolution members got to vote on was the one introduced by the Television Committee, and it passed 102 to 71.

Though its resolution was adopted at the 1955 convention, the Television Committee felt increased pressure to include regional broadcasts in its 1955 plan. One result of this pressure was that the committee took longer than usual to formulate the actual plan. Responding to those who believed that regional broadcasts would stimulate interest in local teams and perhaps even increase ticket sales, the Television Committee devised a plan that called for eight Saturdays of one national broadcast and five Saturdays of regional broadcasts. The plan included another attempt to capitalize on regional interest. It was called "the 400-mile exception," and it allowed

a game played 400 miles or more away from the visiting team's campus to be released for telecast in the visiting college's home television station area ... provided that such arrangement would do no harm to any other game occurring simultaneously in that same area.[48]

When the Big Ten meeting of athletic directors and faculty representatives voted to recommend approval of this plan, harmony returned to the Association. Because the final NCAA plan included many of the provisions lobbied for at the annual convention, it passed easily in a mail vote, 193 to 27.

On March 26, 1955, the NCAA awarded its television contract to NBC, which had been competing vigorously with CBS. NBC got the rights to broadcast on the eight national dates, but under the provisions of the NCAA's plan, which allowed the teams featured on the regional broadcasts to negotiate their television rights, NBC found it had to compete with other stations for regional contracts. Nonetheless, under the complicated national-regional plan used in the fall of 1955, 124 teams appeared on television, and attendance rose 3.3 percent over the 1954 season, to 14.5 million.[49]

Because its 1955 television plan had worked so well, the Television Committee moved to adopt a plan similar to it for use in 1956. The Television Committee's general resolution, which called for the study of television, the formation of recommendations, and the prohibition of television commitments until the next NCAA television policy appeared in the mail, passed with no debate. Not even Notre Dame and the University of Pennsylvania objected to a plan that allowed them to broadcast occasionally on a regional basis and regain at least some of the revenue they had lost under earlier NCAA plans.

The specific television plan sent out in the spring of 1956 passed 224 to 12, and NORC reported in January of 1957 that this policy had produced a 5 percent increase in overall attendance during the 1956 season. Furthermore, NORC reported that

games facing no TV competition were 8 percent better off than those games facing television competition.

Games facing the distant television teams were 8 percent better off than games facing regional competition.

Regional TV hurts the most, with average attendance off 16 percent from the average game facing no TV competition at all.[50]

Because the 1956 television plan had been so successful (despite the bit of bad news about regional telecasting), the Television Committee had little problem passing its general resolution for its 1957 plan at the next convention.

During 1957, the specific television plan was adopted by a mail vote of 212 to 4. The plan called for eight national broadcasting dates and four regional dates. In return, as much as $85,000 went to the two schools that competed on a national broadcast, and $80,000 went to the two schools that appeared on a regional telecast. Attendance increased 2.7 percent during the 1957 season.[51]

Though its broadcast plans had remained basically unchanged over the preceding four years, in 1957 the NCAA began to reserve television time to deliver a series of special "halftime messages." At the half of all its football games, the NCAA superimposed its seal on the screen while an announcer intoned an informative message highlighting the Association's growth, its emphasis on academics, its commitment to safe rules, its national championship tournaments, or its enforcement of rules requiring proper conduct in intercollegiate sports.

These messages portrayed the NCAA as a positive force in college sports unmotivated by economic self-interest. As such, and inserted among waving flags and marching bands, the messages increased the NCAA's stock of goodwill and thickened the smokescreen behind which it enacted restrictive measures that might have been challenged legally. Constant public reminders that it had only the welfare of college sports at heart allowed the NCAA to proceed unchecked in its many restrictive enterprises.

By 1960, NCAA football was enjoying such record attendance levels that the adoption of an annual television policy caused none of the problems it once had. In fact, in 1960 the NCAA decided to economize by adopting a television plan and awarding contracts over a two-year period.

THE NCAA AND CONTROL OVER
POSTSEASON COMPETITION

The NCAA's other, but less troublesome, problem after World War II was a proliferation of postseason football bowl games. Though the promoters of these games generally emphasized their charitable contributions, the NCAA actually knew little about them and grew concerned, as their number increased, that improprieties might be taking place. The NCAA was also, and not just incidentally, concerned to see that its member schools received a fair share of the bowl proceeds. To learn more about the financial arrangements of each bowl game, the NCAA sent a questionnaire to the sponsors of 30 bowls held in early 1947. Only 16 returned the questionnaires.

The information in the responses revealed that while some bowl games did support charity, most returned a significant portion of their profits to their sponsors. The 16 respondents reported total gate receipts of $1,500,727.78 and an after-expense revenue of $202,569.46.[52] All games reported a profit except the 1947 Will Rogers Bowl, which lost $11,145.[53] In spite of this information, many questions remained about the motives of the sponsors, the amount of money the schools received, and those who did not respond to the first questionnaire. Thus, the NCAA sent out another questionnaire in 1948.

Only 17 of the (this time) 50 bowl game sponsors surveyed responded to the inquiry into financial arrangements with the invited school. From the responses, the NCAA learned that the percentage of the bowl revenue devolving to the schools themselves varied from 86 to 33 percent.[54] The renewed reluctance of the remaining 33 sponsors to report the relevant financial data also aroused some suspicion within the Association committee that conducted the survey; it concluded that an insufficient share was reaching the bowl game participants. Their report recommended, and the members agreed, that no NCAA school commit to a bowl game after the postseason of 1950. In addition, the NCAA authorized this committee to recommend a national postseason competition policy.

The committee (known now as the Bowl Game Committee) reported to the next convention and recommended a constitutional amendment covering all aspects of the postseason competition. This code, "Principles Governing Competition in Post-Season and Non-College Sponsored Contests," was adopted by the membership at the convention. It established strict rules governing the appearance of NCAA members in any postseason football game and limited a school to one postseason appearance. It dictated the number of tickets participating schools would receive, and, most important, the code specified that game revenues were to be divided 75 percent to the competing institutions and 25 percent to the sponsor. Finally, the code also required that the sponsors of postseason games invite NCAA representatives to serve on their boards.

To enforce these rules, the NCAA established a Committee on Extra Events. Its primary responsibility was to certify that the sponsors of a bowl game complied with these new rules.

In contrast to other NCAA regulatory efforts, which were couched in public service terms, this move to control postseason football represented perhaps the most open maneuver to transfer income to its members. Despite some brief discussion about "protecting student-athletes from injury," no interpretation of this plan, except as an attempt to divert income from bowl game sponsors to the NCAA members, bears scrutiny. Indeed, the NCAA was so determined to ensure that the schools collected their share of all money generated by a postseason contest that it went on to define what revenue should be available to its members. According to the NCAA, the participant's share was to come from

all revenue derived from the game including sale of tickets (less taxes), concessions, programs, radio rights, video rights, movie rights, and any other income derived from the operation of the game. Any complimentary tickets shall be accounted for at face value and shall become a part of the gross receipts.[55]

The NCAA would make its postseason plan work by certifying postseason games. With a rule allowing a team only one postseason football appearance a year and its ability to certify games, the NCAA could effectively control the number of annual bowl games. Since public demand for these games was high, if the NCAA were to limit or even decrease their number by certifying fewer games, these contests would generate more money. Based on the NCAA's rules governing revenue distribution, larger game proceeds naturally provided more money to the participating schools.

Not surprisingly, the NCAA used this power to reduce the number of bowl games. At the 1953 convention, the Committee on Extra Events reported that in 1951 11 games were certified and in 1952 only 9 games had been certified.[56] Recalling that in the late 1940s as many as 50 bowl games had been played, we see yet another similarity between the NCAA activity and cartel theory. With its ceritification and new rules limiting appearances, the NCAA restricted the number of postseason games, which cartel theory supposes to produce an increase in the revenue paid to the participants. By adopting this postseason competition policy, the NCAA took an official and open step to limit industry output and increase the payments to the participants in postseason games.

By the mid-1950s this process worked so smoothly that the Extra Events Committee gave only a short report to each annual convention in which it repeated its list of certified postseason games.

NOTES

1. Joseph N. Kane, *Famous First Facts* (New York: H. W. Wilson, 1981), 647.
2. Ibid., 121.
3. Ibid., 123.

4. Ibid., 126.

5. Ibid., 132.

6. Ibid., 133-34.

7. *Proceedings of the National Collegiate Athletic Association*, 1949, 113-14. (hereafter cited as *NCAA Proceedings*).

8. Ibid., 114-115.

9. Ibid., 115.

10. Ibid., 116.

11. Ibid., 121.

12. Ibid.

13. 1950 *NCAA Proceedings*, 101.

14. 1949 *NCAA Proceedings*, 108.

15. Ibid., 117.

16. Ibid., 118.

17. Ibid., 119-20.

18. 1951 *NCAA Proceedings*, 34.

19. Ibid., 45.

20. 1950 *NCAA Proceedings*, 124.

21. Home-and-home arrangements are agreements between schools to play each other for two years, one year at each school's home field.

22. 1951 *NCAA Proceedings*, 145.

23. Ibid., 203.

24. For the exact description of the plan see 1952 *NCAA Proceedings*, 154.

25. Among the bidders were the Chevrolet Motor Company, the Atlantic Richfield Company, the Westinghouse Electric Company, the National Broadcasting Company, and the Dumont Television Network.

26. 1952 *NCAA Proceedings*, 155.

27. Kane, *Famous First Facts*, 646-47.

28. This was an ideal game for attracting appreciative spectators. Michigan State was ranked ninth in the nation by the final Associated Press Poll in 1950 and would end the 1951 season ranked second. Notre Dame, always the fans' favorite, had ended the 1949 season ranked first.

29. 1952 *NCAA Proceedings*, 157.

30. See Shirley Povich, "NCAA Messes Up Its Football TV Program," *Washington Post*, November 8, 1951, 20.

31. Ibid., 158.

32. In theater television, fans paid a fee to enter a movie theater and see the live broadcast of a football game.

33. Attendance at all college games fell by 7.8 percent. See *Report of the NCAA Television Committee* (Shawnee Mission, Kans.: NCAA, 1969), 39.

34. 1952 *NCAA Proceedings*, 166-67.

35. Ibid., 213-14.

36. "Big Losses Cited," *New York Times*, Jan. 4, 1953, sec. 5, 4.

37. "TV Fees Hit $1,151,109," *New York Times*, March 23, 1953, 29.

38. 1969 *Report of the NCAA Television Committee*, 39.

39. 1953 *NCAA Proceedings*, 169.

40. Ibid., 170.

41. Ibid., 171.

42. This list appears in "Notre Dame Hits Controlled Video," *New York Times*, Jan. 4, 1953, sec. 5, 1.

43. 1953 *NCAA Proceedings*, 179.

44. 1954 *NCAA Proceedings*, 208.

45. Ibid., 210.

46. 1969 *Report of the NCAA Television Committee*, 39.

47. Ibid., 39.

48. 1956 *NCAA Proceedings*, 207-8.

49. Ibid., 210.

50. 1957 *NCAA Proceedings*, 227-28.

51. 1958 *NCAA Proceedings*, 187.

52. 1948 *NCAA Proceedings*, 183. These bowl games, listed by game, location, and sponsor, answered the questionnaires:

Rose Bowl, Pasadena, Calif., Pacific Athletic Conference;
Shrine East-West All-Star, San Francisco, Calif., Shrine Temple;
Will Rogers Bowl Classic, Oklahoma City, Okla., Veterans of Foreign Wars;
Sun Bowl, El Paso, Tex., Southern Sun Carnival Association, directors are members of various service clubs;
Cotton Bowl, Dallas, Tex., Houston Chamber of Commerce;
Raisin Bowl, Fresno, Calif., Fresno Junior Chamber of Commerce;
Sugar Bowl, New Orleans, La., New Orleans Mid-Winter Sports Association, a civic organization composed of 39 businessmen;
Tampa Cigar Bowl, Tampa, Fla., Egypt Temple Shrine;
Orange Bowl, Miami, Fla., Orange Bowl Committee, an organization of 42 Florida-minded men;
Gator Bowl, Jacksonville, Fla., Gator Bowl Association, an organization of local businessmen;
Tangerine Bowl, Orlando, Fla., Benevolent and Protective Order of Elks;
Pineapple Bowl, Honolulu, Hawaii, University of Hawaii;
Glass Bowl, Toledo, Ohio., University of Toledo;
Alamo Bowl, San Antonio, Tex., Benevolent and Protective Order of Elks; and
Harbor Bowl, San Diego, Calif., San Diego Chamber of Commerce.

53. 1948 *NCAA Proceedings*, 183-84.

54. 1949 *NCAA Proceedings*, 169. The Cotton Bowl reported that it paid the two schools that participated 75 percent of the gross receipts; the Rose Bowl, 70 percent; the Sugar Bowl, 55 percent; the Orange Bowl, 38 percent; the Salad Bowl, 86 percent; the Glass Bowl, 85 percent; the Pear Bowl, 82 percent; the Tangerine Bowl, 76 percent; the Gator Bowl, 70 percent; the Sun Bowl, 67 percent; the Gold Dust Bowl, 56 percent; the Raisin Bowl, 47 percent; the Burley Bowl, 40 percent; and the Junior Rose Bowl, 33 percent.

55. Ibid., 269.

56. 1953 *NCAA Proceedings*, 225.

CHAPTER 4

Division Within the Intercollegiate Athletic Cartel, 1960-85

By the beginning of the 1960s, the National Collegiate Athletic Association (NCAA) found itself comfortably in control of college athletics. With widespread support from the membership, it actively enforced rules and punished violators. And, through its Television Committee, it organized and negotiated the revenue-enhancing television contract.

During the period traced here, the NCAA continued to restrict competition for athletes, limit their compensation, reduce the expenses required to field sports teams, and sell broadcast rights collectively. As the Association grew, however, the diversity in its membership's athletic emphases began to cause problems that finally led to reorganization of the Association, grouping like-minded athletic interests (first into Divisions I,II, and III, then into I-A, I-AA, II, and III). But even this periodic division could not stop the inevitable problems that all cartels face.

TELEVISION AND THE REORGANIZATION OF THE NCAA

From the very start, the NCAA had been aware of the direct and potentially crippling competition professional football presented for college football. The largest form of this competition came by way of television, which forced football fans to choose between attending or viewing a college or professional game. To ensure its members the greatest possible financial return, the NCAA had to eliminate such a dangerous choice. Unfortunately, the NCAA had no control over professional football's television policy; moveover, the pros proved reluctant to alter their own, lucrative television policy. Incredibly, the U.S. Congress enacted as a consequence a federal law effectively restricting any competitive televising of professional and college football games.

In July 1961, for the second time in less than a decade, the NFL's practice of negotiating a collective television contract was ruled to violate antitrust law because it eliminated competition for the sale of television rights. As a result, in the fall of 1961, the NFL owners convinced New York Congressman Emanuel Cellar, Chairman of the House Judiciary Committee, to introduce a bill to exempt professional football teams (and other sports) from the Sherman Antitrust Act and to allow them to negotiate television contracts collectively. The text of Cellar's bill (H. R. 8757) stated that

the antitrust laws, as defined [in U.S. Code], shall not apply to any joint agreement by or among persons engaging in or conducting the organized professional team sports of football, . . . by which a league of clubs . . . sells or otherwise transfers all or any part of the rights of such league's members clubs in the sponsored telecasting of the games.[1]

Noticing in this legislative maneuvering an excellent opportunity to limit television competition from professional football, the NCAA sent William Reed, its Legislative Committee Chairman, and committee member Asa Bushnell of the ECAC, to the committee hearings. Reed surmised that, as written, H.R. 8757 would adversely affect his membership unless the committee amended the bill to provide that

the [broadcasting of] organized professional football from telecasting stations located within 75 miles of the game site chosen by a college or university on a day other than Sunday, when such college or university is scheduled to play there an intercollegiate contest in football, shall be unlawful.[2]

Cloaked in the mantle of altruism, the NCAA amendment would limit pro football competition for the spectator's dollar and assign the Justice Department to enforce this limit. With no choice between a college game and a televised professional game, a good many fans, the NCAA reasoned, would attend college games and swell their gate receipts. After some changes in its wording, including an extension of the period during which a professional game could not be broadcast without the team losing its antitrust exemption, the Cellar bill, complete with the NCAA's interpolation, became law on September 30, 1961.

In early 1962, the NCAA sold the football broadcast rights to the 1962 and 1963 seasons to CBS for $5.1 million per year. In the Association's mail referendum that spring, the contract was approved 178 to 62, and while the 178 yes votes exceeded 160 votes necessary for approval, the 62 no votes represented the largest negative response the NCAA's television plan had yet received.

The unsettling results of this vote indicated that not a few nonappearing schools were disenchanted with the division of the television spoils. Some of them had quietly begun a campaign for a more equitable share-the-wealth approach. This share-the-wealth idea, first softly mentioned a decade earlier, included a set fee to be paid for a television appearance and a distribution of the balance among those members that made no television appearances.

CBS, in fact, gave careful consideration to a share-the-wealth procedure, and at one point, it planned to allocate $4.35 million to schools that played on television games and to divide the remaining $750,000 among the other NCAA members, giving each school approximately $18,000. After observing the legal problems professional football encountered with a collective provision, CBS decided not to risk similar problems and never seriously pursued this provision.

The Association's difficulties in deciding how to divide the television money, however, were becoming more apparent. The smaller schools that did not appear on television wanted a larger share of the television money; the larger schools that did appear on television and earned the money had no desire to share it. Bill Flynn, Boston College athletic director and chairman of the NCAA Television Committee, was typical of those members who believed the solution was a wider distribution of television receipts. He recommended that a study be conducted to determine legal methods to "enable more of the colleges . . . to share at least modestly in the tangible returns from the NCAA television program."[3]

The problems confronting the decision-making ability of the NCAA come as no surprise if traditional cartel theory is applied. When the members of a cartel attempt to reach agreement on how the cartel operates (that is, how it controls output, price, market division, and the division of the profits), they are forced to make collective decisions. This decision-making process is less expensive when all members are equally efficient (in terms of incurring costs) at fielding football teams because the members are more willing to agree on policies that affect them all the same way. Put another way, when all the cartel members have the same football desires, a policy that increases the profits of one member is readily accepted by all the members.

If, however, the members have different football desires and some can control costs better than others, decision making often becomes difficult. When members have different objectives, a policy that increases the profits of one firm may not be approved by those firms whose profits do not likewise increase. Thus, with members whose goals and methods differ, the process of making collective decisions tends to become difficult and costly.

As a cartel, the NCAA encountered this problem throughout the 1960s and the 1970s. When members of the NCAA decided on a television contract, they were actually dividing the rents they earned by agreeing to restrict television broadcasts.[4] That is, the large sums the NCAA generated by restricting broadcasts were distributed to those schools with football teams proficient enough to have their games selected for television. But while all members were asked to forego unsanctioned television appearances, not all members shared in the rewards this sacrifice brought. The few schools that appeared on television appreciated the way the Association divided the television revenue, but those who did not appear on television did not share this enthusiasm. A negative vote in the television referendum was one way to register this dissatisfaction and, therefore, the results of the 1962 vote indicate a growing unhappiness with the method the NCAA used to divide the television money.

At the 1964 convention, the Television Committee announced that it had contracted with NBC to televise the 1964 and 1965 college football seasons. The two-year NBC television contract paid the Association $6,522,000 for the rights to broadcast 29 college games in 1964. During the 1964 season, live football attendance recorded its largest increase since the NCAA began keeping records in 1947: 5.02 percent over 1963, a record increase of 1,117,383 fans. The highest rated broadcast of the season was Army's November 28th 11-to-8 victory over Navy, which reached an estimated 16.2 million television fans.

In 1965, NBC broadcast 32 college games and again, an attendance record was set when ticket sales increased by 5.69 percent (or 1,328, 095) to 24,682,572. Also in 1965, the Television Committee sold the broadcast rights for the 1966 and 1967 college football seasons for a total of 15.5 million, along with an option for ABC to renew the agreement for two more seasons for an additional $16.7 million.[5] This option was exercised by ABC; the network eventually purchased the broadcast rights for the 1971 and 1972 seasons for $24 million and the television rights for the 1972 and 1973 seasons for $27 million.

While college football continued to be profitable for the NCAA as a whole, as evidenced by the increasing revenue generated by the sale of the broadcast rights, NCAA members who seldom appeared on television faced financial difficulties. These financial problems fell disproportionately on smaller schools, which were less equipped to absorb the expenses of football, and many of them dropped the sport to save money. Marquette University dropped football in December 1960 after its program lost $50,000 in the 1960 season. Bradley dropped football in December 1970, citing economic reasons. In 1971, the State University of Buffalo dropped football after it had sustained losses of $400,000 over the previous four years. And, within one month of each other in late 1973, first Drexel, then Xavier University (located in Cincinnati) announced they were dropping football after fielding teams since 1919 and 1900, respectively. In all, 41 schools dropped football in the 1963-73 decade.

Still the tension caused by the television revenue split and the different sports ambitions of the members continued to mount. After two years of frequently debating how to address the problem, the NCAA held a special summer convention in August 1973, during which the Association reorganized its membership. Already a diverse group when it came to athletic goals and skills, the NCAA decided to organize into three divisions, attempting to place schools of similar athletic aspirations in the same division.

Division I included the large schools—such as Penn State, Notre Dame, and Oklahoma—that operated big-time athletic programs. Division II included somewhat smaller schools, like the University of Puget Sound and South Dakota State, that aspired to big-time programs but lacked the resources to implement them. Division III included the small colleges, like Washingon and Lee and Case Western Reserve, that maintained athletic programs but did not field highly competitive teams. Within their divisions, the members were allowed to make some division-binding decisions on such practices as financial aid and recruiting. The Association as a whole, however, voted on other issues.

After the summer convention of 1973, the 667 members were divided so that 234 schools were categorized in Division III and 194 went into Division II. The membership of Division I was less straightforward because an initial 124 schools were included and an additional 111 were categorized as Division I in all sports except football. Thus, Division I had 235 members, of whom only 124 had football programs, some of these with greater ambitions than records.

At the annual convention of 1974, the Television Committee announced that the contract it had negotiated with ABC for $15.85 million a season for the 1974 and 1975 seasons had been approved in a mail referendum vote 300 to 10. Under the provisions of this contract, ABC would present 20 games, with a national appearance bringing $488,000, split between the two teams, compared with $431,000 per game under the previous contract. A regional game would bring $355,000 (compared with $315,000). In a special arrangement designed to appease those schools that had reluctantly moved to the other divisions, ABC also agreed to televise the NCAA Division II semifinal and championship football games and the Division III football championship.[6]

At the Association's special 1975 summer convention devoted to the economics of intercollegiate sports, however, the members continued to focus on the division of television revenue. Stephen Horn, President of California State University, Long Beach, proposed that television revenue be divided among all those NCAA members that played football rather than just the schools that appeared on television. Under Horn's plan, 15 percent of the television money would go to televised schools and the remainder would be divided 50 percent for Division I, 25 percent for Division II, and 25 percent for Division III.

Horn's plan naturally appealed to the smaller schools that never appeared on television, but it was anathema to the Division I schools, which would earn only $46,000 for a television appearance instead of the 1975 fee, nearly six times as large. The football powerhouses, fearing the redistribution of wealth that would take place under this proposal, referred to Horn's proposal as the "Robin Hood proposal."

Undeterred, Horn went on to propose a similar redistribution of the money produced by postseason bowl games: 50 percent to be divided between the participating schools, 25 percent to the rest of the Division I schools, and 12.5 percent each to Divisions II and III. This plan also appealed to many smaller schools but almost completely alienated the large schools.

Because the special summer convention of 1975 was called explicitly to discuss methods to reduce expenditures, it was deemed inappropriate to consider Horn's motions at that time. Instead, both of his proposals were considered at the regular convention of 1976.

At that convention, Horn's proposal to divide the bowl receipts was ruled out of order because the Association felt it inappropriate to consider a motion concerning division of money between a bowl and the schools. While the NCAA had rules governing the percentage of the bowl receipts a school could receive, it resisted involvement in what was essentially a private contractual agreement between the bowl and the school. Thus, NCAA President John A. Fuzak, presiding over the meeting, refused to consider Horn's bowl proposal. Horn appealed Fuzak's decision but it was upheld by the convention.

Horn's television proposal required the approval of the entire Association because money was to be redistributed to all three divisions. While some small schools supported the motion, it was soundly defeated. No doubt some members of the NCAA were affected by the threats of the big-time schools who, since the appearance of Horn's motion the previous summer, had been talking about leaving the Association if it passed. Nonetheless, the Robin Hood proposal gave the larger schools some food for thought: As long as the NCAA followed the one-school, one-vote procedure for its collective decisions, it would be theoretically possible for the more numerous smaller schools to redistribute resources from the larger schools to themselves. They had tried and failed in 1976, but they might try again.

In a related matter at the 1976 convention, the members returned to the issue of voting procedures. Since 1973, when the Association had divided into three membership divisions and the schools had been required to vote with their respective divisions, problems had arisen over the voting arrangements for those members who maintained football or basketball teams that played in divisions different from those of the rest of the school's teams. The most frequent occurrence of this was a school that did not play football but voted with Division I on basketball issues and with another division for other sports questions. The NCAA Council proposed that members vote entirely with the division in which their football or basketball team played. Both Division II and Division III approved this legislation, but Divison I did not. And since the vote required the approval of all three divisions, Division I's vote defeated the measure.

Division I defeated the voting measure because the football schools in the division did not want to share voting in their division with schools not philosophically committed, in terms of overall size and the goals of their entire athletic program, to Division I. The big schools realized that, given a chance to vote on certain financial issues, these other schools would not necessarily align themselves with the rest of Division I. Hence, Division I defeated the rule that would have allowed nonfootball schools, primarily those who could qualify because of their basketball team, to vote in their division.

Talk of further reorganizing the NCAA's top division appeared after the 1976 convention. The schools committed to highly competitive nationally recognized football programs wanted more control over Division I and backed plans to remove the less committed schools from the division. In the spring, a plan to cut the division from 138 to 97 members was made public. It drew instant criticism from the larger football schools because it did not reduce the division enough and from the less ambitious schools because they considered it too drastic a cut. The NCAA quickly backed away from the plan, saying it was only a draft proposal in its preliminary stages.

But the controversy surrounding reorganization continued. In September 1976, the Council officially stated that it would sponsor no reorganization plan that year. But at the annual convention in January 1977, NCAA Executive Director Walter Byers was quoted as saying, "I see reorganization as necessary and inevitable."[7] Nonetheless, the convention rejected all reorganization plans.

On December 20, 1976, representatives from 56 big-time football schools held a meeting in the Dallas-Fort Worth Marina Hotel at which they expressed common complaints about the way the NCAA handled their problems. Those in attendance decided to form a group for only those NCAA members with major football programs. The criteria they outlined at that time included (1) a stadium seating at least 30,000, (2) average home game attendance over the last three years of 20,000, and (3) a schedule that included a minimum of 70 percent of the contests against other members of the group.

Out of this meeting came the idea of the College Football Association (CFA), and the invitations to join it were sent out to 78 schools in January 1977. The first official meeting of the group occurred on July 5, 1977, in Atlanta, where the members formalized their proposals for reorganizing Division I. (The 61 schools that joined the CFA are listed in Appendix D.) Ironically, this meeting took place shortly before the NCAA announced that it had sold the television rights for the 1978 through 1981 seasons to ABC for the largest amount ever—$116 million.

During the last half of 1977, CFA members repeatedly called for the reorganization of the NCAA's Division I. Finally, at the 1978 convention, the Association reorganized Division I into Division I-A and Division I-AA. As the reorganization was initially envisioned, Division I-A would consist of the larger schools that maintained nationally competitive football programs, and I-AA would consist of schools that played major but not truly big-time football.

The NCAA established four criteria for I-A membership. A university (1) had to maintain at least eight varsity intercollegiate sports, including football; (2) had to schedule at least 60 percent of its football games against Division I-A opponents; (3) had to have averaged 17,000 paid attendance at all home games from 1974 through 1977; and (4) had to use a stadium for home games with a minimum of 30,000 permanent seats.

The attendance criterion caused the largest controversy. Without it, almost all Division I schools could have qualified for Division I-A. With it, however, a good many schools would be forced into Division I-AA. The nation's football factories appreciated this requirement because fewer schools in Division I-A meant more television money per member. In fact, they had hoped that this clause would be used to reduce the membership in Division I-A to 79 schools.

Meanwhile, the schools that would be consigned to Division I-AA saw that the passage of these Division I-A requirements would deny them both television money and the votes to reverse the denial. A small group of these schools, led by the Ivy League, suggested an amendment that would exempt schools that fielded 12 sports from the attendance requirements. Andrew Geiger, athletic director at the University of Pennsylvania, introduced this amendment, which became known as the Ivy League amendment. It narrowly passed 73 to 70, but had the important effect of letting schools that did not field nationally competitive football teams, like Appalachian State, Ohio University, and Ball State, into Division I-A.

Even with the Ivy League amendment, the decision to split Division I-A was a close one. An 82-73 roll call vote indicated a good deal of lingering concern about the plan, especially among those schools who would benefit from the Ivy League amendment. Ironically, after this reorganization, Division I-A consisted of 137 schools, compared with the 142 schools that had belonged to the old Division I.

The larger football schools, most of whom belonged to the CFA, were not pleased by the decision to keep so many schools in Division I-A. At the 1979 convention they tried to reduce the size of the newly created top division by repealing the Ivy League amendment. Their attempt came up on the short side of an 83-64 vote.

As the 1980s began, the CFA members made it clear they were not content with size of Division I-A and their resulting share of the television revenue. Rather than make periodic (although frequent, by NCAA standards) appearances in the NCAA plan, these schools felt they should enjoy the "property right" to their broadcasts. In January 1981 the CFA members passed, in a 44-12 vote, a resolution declaring that

the CFA members reserve unto themselves the right to determine the best use of their property rights to broadcast, telecast and cable cast their members' institutional football contests.[8]

On July 19, the CFA board of directors presented plans to representatives of NBC and ABC for a television contract involving only its members. The NCAA, they argued, was including so many non-CFA members in its plan that ratings were dropping. They proposed an alternative, non-NCAA contract.

Less than two weeks after this meeting, the NCAA announced that it had signed a television contract for the 1982 through 1985 seasons. Under this four-year pact with two networks, CBS and ABC, instead of the traditional one network, the NCAA would collect $264 million for the broadcast rights. Teams playing on a nationally televised game would divide $1 million in 1982, increasing to $1.5 million in 1985. A regional appearance started at $700,000 and grew to $800,000 over the same period. In addition, the NCAA signed a separate agreement with the Turner Broadcasting System (TBS), which paid the NCAA $17.5 million for the right to televise 19 games in both the 1982 and 1983 seasons.

The new NCAA-ABC-CBS-TBS agreements sought to assuage many of the complaints of the major football schools by increasing the number of times they could appear on television each season. Under the new agreements, a school could appear on television three times during the regular season, with two of those appearances being national games. Interestingly, the NCAA-ABC-CBS contract contained a special clause which called for renegotiations if the CFA schools were unavailable.

Even with the increased appearances and payments that would more than double those of the previous contract, the CFA members did not wholeheartedly support the NCAA agreement. Complaining that they were really guaranteed no appearances, the CFA members voted 33-20 on August 21, 1981, to tentatively approve a four-year television contract with NBC, under which NBC would pay the CFA $180 million for the broadcast rights to their games. In contrast to the NCAA-ABC-CBS-TBS plans, each CFA member was guaranteed $1 million worth of appearances every two years. CFA members were given until September 10 to decide which television plan, CFA or NCAA, they would play under.

After the CFA-NBC contract was initialled, prominent members of the NCAA (Executive Director Walter Byers, Assistant Executive Director Thomas Hansen, NCAA President James Frank, and Charles Alan Wright, chairman of the NCAA Infractions Committee) let it be known that any NCAA member who televised their games outside of NCAA's television plan would be quickly and severely penalized. The CFA got an injunction against this threatened behavior on September 8, 1981, and the Universities of Georgia and Oklahoma (together) and the University of Texas sued the NCAA, charging that its control of television was an antitrust violation. Just prior to the September 10 deadline, the NCAA announced it would hold a special convention in December 1981 to resolve the television problem. With all this activity surrounding television and the call for a special convention, the CFA postponed its deadline until December 15. Similarly, the courts agreed to delay hearing the three universities' cases until after the December convention.

As the special convention approached, the NCAA announced that it would not consider the question of who owned the television rights at that convention. This decision prompted the court hearing the Georgia and Oklahoma suit to announce that it would continue as scheduled. In November, the case was put back on track when both sides were ordered to prepare their cases.

In December, the special convention of the NCAA decided to trim the number of members in Division I-A by including an attendance requirement similar to the one rejected almost four years earlier. Under the new agreement, which would take effect on September 1, 1982, Division I-A membership would require schools to have averaged 17,000 paid spectators per home game over the last four years and to have stadiums with at least 30,000 seats.

This new requirement decreased the number of Division I-A members to 92. It also split several conferences, with some members meeting the new qualifications to remain in Division I-A, while other members could not meet the criterion and were relegated to Division I-AA. The Ivy League was one such conference, with only Yale meeting the requirements for Division I-A. Yale, however, chose to drop to Division I-AA with the rest of the conference.

The extended December 15 deadline for CFA members to choose between the NCAA television contract and the alternative one offered by NBC passed with an insufficient number of schools opting for the NBC deal, voiding the CFA-NBC agreement. But the question of who owned the television broadcast rights remained unanswered in minds of many, and it was put before the entire Association at the 1982 annual convention. Prior to the convention, the members of the CFA had Judge Herman Jones of the Travis County District Court in Texas issue an injunction blocking this vote. However, another judge in the same court blocked Jones's injunction, and the NCAA members voted overwhelmingly in support of this motion:

The Association shall control all forms of the telecasting, cablecasting or otherwise televising of the intercollegiate football games of member institutions during the traditional fall seasons.[9]

Nonetheless, the litigation against the NCAA over television rights continued into 1982. On July 7, 1982, the NCAA went to trial in U.S. District Court in Oklahoma in the antitrust suit brought by the Board of Regents of the University of Oklahoma and the University of Georgia Athletic Association.[10] The trial lasted until July 15, and Judge Juan Burciaga of New Mexico (presiding because the local judges had withdrawn) delivered his opinion on September 15, 1982.

(While Burciaga deliberated, the case filed separately by the University of Texas, in the Texas State Court in Austin, was dismissed when the judge decided that Texas had to comply with NCAA rules "as a matter of law." Even with this August 16, 1982, decision, the U.S. Department of Justice announced it would examine the NCAA's television contract for possible antitrust violations.)

Georgia and Oklahoma charged that the NCAA violated the Sherman Antitrust Act because it established the price for football television rights and prevented members from individually selling their broadcasts. At first, the NCAA argued in defense that it was a voluntary association and that the defendants were free to leave and to make broadcast arrangements with any television network. But the court, noting that NCAA membership was necessary for schools desiring to maintain large athletic programs, concluded that

NCAA membership is not voluntary for these plaintiffs or for many other colleges and universities for which athletic excellence is an institutional priority.[11]

Because the charge of price-fixing had been levied against the NCAA, the court also examined how the prices paid for each telecast were determined by the carrying network. This investigation revealed that (during 1978-81) ABC agreed to pay a specific sum for the rights to televise college football (in 1978, $29 million), but it was never stipulated in the contract exactly how this money was to be paid out per television appearance. The NCAA Football Television Committee provided ABC with recommendations about these payments, and ABC always implemented these recommendations to the letter.

In 1978, the price recommendation was made by Thomas Hansen, the NCAA's television program director. He wrote to ABC suggesting that the $29 million be divided as shown in Table 6. A similar method was employed each year until the contract expired at the end of the 1981 season.

The NCAA argued that each school could negotiate with the network, but the court noted that an individual school had no influence over a network offer. If the school did not accept the offer, NCAA rules precluded it from approaching another network. Further, if the school caused ABC too many problems, the network would simply televise another game. Thus, the court called this supposed option to negotiate "illusory."[12]

As an example of how the NCAA's television control altered the free market process, the court recalled what took place the previous fall when both the Oklahoma-USC and the Appalachian State-Citadel games had been televised. More than 200 stations had picked up the Oklahoma game, but only 4 carried Appalachian State. Yet each school received the same payment:

The evidence is also clear that some teams would have received larger fees were they allowed to negotiate with any and all potential broadcasters. At the

Table 6
Dividing ABC's 1978 Aggregate Television Payment

Fee	Event
$750,000	Division I-A Playoffs
$670,000	Division II, III Playoffs
$165,000	Regular Telecasts, Divisions II, III
$250,000	Other Championship Events
$1,835,000	[Non-Division I Subtotal]
$2,173,200	8% NCAA Assessment on $27,165,000 (Total less 4 payments above)
$6,939,800	Payment for National Telecasts (13 games at $533,600 each)
$18,054,990	Payment for Regional Telecasts (45 games at $401,222 each)
$27,164,999	[Division I Subtotal]
$28,999,990	Total Payment (Payment was to be $29 million)

Source: *Board of Regents v. NCAA*, 546 F. Supp. 1276 (1982).

same time, the testimony made clear that many of the smaller schools would not have received as much as they did under the NCAA plans if they were forced to compete in a free market.[13]

What made the price fixing so rewarding, according to the court, was the NCAA's exclusive agreement with the network. The network was willing to pay a large sum for exclusive rights, which the Association ensured by preventing any effective competition. The court concluded that to ensure this exclusivity, the NCAA had "agreed to limit production to a level far below that which would occur in a free market situation."[14]

The NCAA defended its policy as necessary in order to protect livegate attendance, which the Association believed would decline if unlimited television broadcasting occurred. The court refused to accept this contention because the NCAA could produce no persuasive evidence to support its belief. The last study conducted by NORC, which had produced the pioneering studies the NCAA used as the basis for its first television policy, had occurred in 1957, and the court found as a matter of law that the techniques used in that study were outdated and incomplete.

In addition, the court could not accept the live-gate argument in light of the fact that the 1982-85 television contract presented an already enormous number of television football hours. Under that contract, nine hours of televised football would be presented almost every autumn Saturday. The belief that increased televising of college football games somehow maintained in-person attendance simply made no sense, and on this point the court ruled that

the NCAA's argument regarding gate attendance is either an ill-founded belief at best, or at worst, a deception employed to make the majority of the NCAA membership believe that they should control television out of self interest.[15]

Accordingly, the court ruled that the "essence of the NCAA controls—indeed their raison d'être—is to restrict competition,"[16] and it judged the NCAA's price-fixing techniques to be a violation of the Sherman Antitrust Act. In conclusion, the court observed that the

controls over college football make the NCAA a classic cartel. Like all other cartels, NCAA members have sought and achieved a price for their product which is, in most instances, artificially high. The NCAA cartel imposes production limits on its members, and maintains mechanisms for punishing cartel members who seek to stray from these production quotas.[17]

As judgment against the NCAA, the court declared the Association's 1982-85 television contract illegal and void. It also directed the Association not to arrange future television contracts. Finally, the district court retained jurisdiction in the matter to monitor compliance.

The NCAA quickly moved to stay (temporarily halt the impact of) the decision while it appealed the ruling. The NCAA first sought a stay from Judge Burciaga, who turned down their request on September 18th. The NCAA turned next to the U.S. Court of Appeals for the Tenth Circuit in Denver. A three-judge panel consisting of James Barrett of Wyoming, James Logan of Kansas, and Stephanie K. Seymour of Oklahoma granted a stay on September 22nd, pending the NCAA's appeal of the decision. The court then gave the NCAA until October 13th to file an appeal and ordered Oklahoma and Georgia to respond by November 3rd. (On November 10th, the U.S. Department of Justice filed a friend of the court brief in support of the case filed by Georgia and Oklahoma.)

The Court of Appeals formed its decision by reconsidering several key points that had been decided by Judge Burciaga, among them:

1. whether the NCAA television plan and contracts constituted price-fixing; and

2. whether the same plan and contracts were unlawful when examined and contrasted with their intended effect.[18]

Regarding the issue of price-fixing, the NCAA argued that the television plan was part of an overall package that included its regulation of athletes and facilities. Further, the NCAA argued once again that restricting television increased gate attendance. But, as in the first decision, the court rejected this point, noting that "an argument that total viewership is enhanced by restricting the sale of broadcast rights is speculative,"[19] and it affirmed the lower court's ruling that

the NCAA television arrangement is so fraught with anticompetitive potential that it appears to be one that would always or almost always tend to restrict competition.[20]

The appeals court went on to examine how the outcome might be affected when NCAA actions were weighed against the Association's intentions, in part because it recognized that a Supreme Court appeal would surely raise this approach on defense. The court reexamined the facts and found that

the television plan is unreasonably restrictive of competitive conditions and therefore unlawful. It increases concentration in the marketplace; it prevents producers from exercising independent pricing and output decisions; it precludes broadcasters from purchasing a product for which there are no readily available substitutes; it facilitates cartelization.[21]

Based on this analysis, the Court of Appeals affirmed the lower court decision by a 2-1 vote on May 12, 1983. The lone dissenter, Justice James Barrett, summarized his views this way:

I firmly believe that to the extent that the NCAA's television restraints upon Oklahoma and Georgia and other member institutions with excellent football programs are anticompetitive, these restraints are fully justified [and] they are necessary to maintain intercollegiate football as amateur competition.[22]

When a rehearing by the appeals court was denied on June 23, 1983, the NCAA appealed to U.S. Supreme Court Justice Byron R. White to stay the rulings of the lower courts until the case could be decided by the Supreme Court. The Association appealed to White because he was the high court justice responsible for matters from the tenth district. Ironically, White had also been a standout halfback at the University of Colorado from 1935 through 1937, earning the nickname "Whizzer." In 1969 he had received the NCAA's top award, the Theodore Roosevelt Award, which is presented annually to the "distinguished citizen . . . [who] exemplifies most clearly the ideals and purposes for which college athletic programs are dedicated."[23] As expected, he stayed the decision on July 15, 1983, allowing the NCAA to continue operating under the agreement signed in 1982 with ABC and CBS.

The Court heard the case on March 20, 1984, and handed down its decision on June 27, 1984.[24] It held that the lower courts had erred when they automatically considered NCAA restrictions to be antitrust violations. To the Court, many of the NCAA rules regarding athletic conduct and governing procedures facilitated the marketing of a product (college football) that might not be readily available otherwise. Said the Court, "[The NCAA] actions widen consumer choice — not only the choices available to sports fans but also those available to athletes — and hence can be viewed as procompetitive."[25]

Thus, the Supreme Court turned to balancing the intent of NCAA rules with their effect and subsequently refused to alter the earlier opinions:

The anticompetitive consequences of this arrangement are apparent. Individual competitors lose their freedom to compete. Price is higher and output lower than they would otherwise be, and both are unresponsive to consumer preference.[26]

Once more the NCAA's justifications for these restrictions underwent examination and once again a court rejected the defense that the NCAA plan protected in-person attendance:

[G]ames are shown on television during all hours that college football games are played. The plan simply does not protect live attendance by ensuring that games will not be shown on television at the same time as live events.[27]

The Court also rejected the NCAA's argument that the television plan helped equalize competition between member schools, and it concluded by agreeing with Judge Burciaga's analysis that more games would reach television without the plan:

The finding that consumption will materially increase if the controls are removed is a compelling demonstration that they do not in fact serve any such legitimate purpose.[28]

In a 7-2 decision, the Court ruled against the NCAA. (Justice White wrote the minority opinion.)

In late October 1984, Judge Burciaga clarified his initial ruling against the NCAA and granted permission to the NCAA to enter the television market to compete against other groups in the sale of football broadcast rights. The NCAA, however, declined.

CONTROLLING COSTS

Freshman Eligibility for Varsity Competition

During World Wars I and II and for one year of the Korean War (1951-52), the NCAA passed special legislation allowing freshman to compete in college athletics. While most able-bodied undergraduates served in the armed forces, this special legislation allowed underaged freshmen to take their places so that colleges could complete their sports schedules free from an interruption in revenue. Shortly after each conflict ended, upperclassmen returned to school and freshmen returned to the sidelines.

Permanent eligibility for freshmen had been seriously discussed in the mid-1950s, but the Executive Committee refused to endorse the idea, believing their participation would interfere with their early studies and the adjustment to college. By the 1967 annual convention, however, the attitude had started to shift toward allowing freshmen to participate. Some argued that 1967 freshmen were more mature than their 1950s predecessors. Others contended that athletics took no more time than such other extracurricular activities as the marching band, in which freshmen were generally allowed to participate.[29] But these points masked the most plausible explanation for the attitude shift that emerges from an examination of the general financial status of college athletic programs in 1967.

In the 1950s, an institution's athletic budget supported fewer sports and commensurately fewer student-athletes than in 1967. But by 1967, the one-year free ride had become a drain on those schools with financial problems. Those schools noticed that freshman eligibility provided them with four years of athletic productivity instead of three for each grant-in-aid they awarded. Hence, they could award fewer grants but gain the same number of student-athlete years of participation.

While the members took no official action at the 1967 convention, an official proposal to make freshmen eligible to compete in varsity sports was presented to the delegates in 1968. This proposal, however, specifically excepted football (and basketball) because its author,

Milton F. Hartvigsen of Brigham Young University, felt that students should not jump into these high-pressure sports as soon as they registered. Little debate over this proposal ensued and it narrowly passed, 163 to 160.

Finally, at the 1972 convention, the Association adopted (by a 94-67 vote) a motion making freshmen eligible for football (and basketball), an adjustment reflecting nothing more than the members' increased attraction to the economic features of freshman eligibility. The Association had been reluctant to adopt freshman eligibility, and as long as its members could afford not to, it resisted. But having established increasing revenue and cost cutting as its principal function, the NCAA simply ignored its once altruistic rationale for keeping freshmen in the classroom and study hall.

The question of freshman eligibility came up again in mid-1983 when a special select NCAA committee headed by John P. Schaefer, former president of the University of Arizona, recommended that freshmen not be eligible to participate in football (and basketball). To offset the reduction in participants such a rule would bring, the committee also recommended that more grants-in-aid be allowed (in Division I, an increase from 95 to 104 for football was recommended). Noting the cost of nine more grants, the NCAA Council did not agree with the committee, and refused to sponsor the recommendation as a proposed amendment at the 1984 annual convention.

Restricting Student-Athlete Compensation

Between 1960 and 1985, the NCAA enacted several measures limiting the compensation provided to college athletes, typically citing its desire to "preserve amateurism." Since the principles of amateurism prohibited schools from paying athletes (though experience indicates that it did not prevent all schools from doing so), schools discovered many ingenious ways to compensate student-athletes indirectly, without exchanging funds. As the NCAA actively enforced amateur rules, it found schools sidestepping the intent of these rules with new methods of rewarding athletes; thus, the NCAA had to write more rules to prevent this behavior. These more extensive and refined rules had the fortunate and not unplanned coincidental effect of decreasing the cost borne by all NCAA members fielding teams.

At the 1961 convention, the members passed (in a 158-46 vote) the amendment now known as the Five-Year Rule, so named because it required student-athletes to complete their three (and later four) years of varsity eligibility in five years. The Five-Year Rule helped members reduce expenditures by limiting the number of years a school could pick up the tab for an athlete on scholarship. Without the rule, schools put athletes on scholarship, allowed them to practice, but held them out of competition, a process known as "redshirting," for years. In this way, wealthier schools could field teams of older, tougher, more experienced student-athletes. With adoption of the Five-Year Rule, however, coaches were only allowed to redshirt athletes for one year, reducing the expense of stockpiling seasoned athletes.

In 1962 the NCAA conducted an extensive examination of the student fees a school had to pay those students on an athletic grant-in-aid, and subsequently, the Council adopted a policy that prohibited schools from paying a student-athlete's test or admission fees, dormitory deposits, uniform fees (if the student-athlete were enrolled in ROTC), and summer school tuition. The Council also issued rules governing the hours worked by and the payment to a student-athlete employed under a grant-in-aid agreement.[30]

These rules effectively decreased athletic department expenditures, standardized the expenses a school could underwrite, and further, prevented the members from using the payment of "incidental fees" as an inducement. Rule refinements like these began to appear frequently in the 1960s, reflecting the Association's efforts to limit the compensation to student-athletes and save its members money.

During 1963, the Council adopted several official interpretations outlining what a school could and could not provide an athlete. One set of official interpretations specified the services a school could provide a student-athlete. Since the NCAA had limited the financial aid awards, some schools had begun to attract athletes by providing them with, among other things, transportation for themselves, their friends, or their families. This subtle form of inducement required the NCAA to formulate detailed rules regarding when and how a school could transport an athlete.[31]

Another interpretation declared any student-athlete who had ever been paid to officiate a game no longer an amateur unless that officiating took place within a school's intramural program.[32] The idea behind this rule was that a student-athlete might be overcompensated unless his officiating occurred in a program that NCAA members could oversee. Similar prohibitions were imposed on the expenses a school could pay if an athlete competed in an event not sponsored by a college.

Meanwhile, even though the NCAA had established complex rules restricting the payments to student-athletes, it came out strongly in 1964 against the player draft in professional sports, complaining that it denied a student-athlete free choice. This was not the first time NCAA members had spoken against the professional draft. Appearing before the Senate Antimonopoly Subcommittee six years earlier, Bud Wilkinson, Duffy Daugherty, and Bowden Wyatt, football coaches at Oklahoma, Michigan State, and Tennessee, respectively, had opposed the draft. Wilkinson in particular articulated the view that professional football was a business and should be treated as such by not allowing the draft:

I have never subscribed to the view that the owners of professional athletics are in business philanthropically, only to provide good times for the American citizen.

My experience is they are quite businesslike, almost ruthless.... They provide recreation for many people, but whenever recreation has begun to conflict with dollar values, I know of very few instances when the expedient dollar avenue was not followed.[33]

In short, refusing to let its members bid competitively for student-athletes because of the expense involved, the Association continued to encourage a competitive athlete allocation process once they left college.

In the mid-1960s, the NCAA took several more steps to reduce athletic department expenditures. Because NCAA regulations limited athlete aid, a student-athlete was often indirectly compensated for his athletic services by working at the summer sports camp run by his coach. The large number of these camps made it difficult for the NCAA to determine what arrangements existed between the athlete and his employer. To reduce the temptation to use summer camp employment as a reward for attending the coach's university, the NCAA enacted lengthy detailed rules governing the athlete's sumer camp compensation.

These rules outlined how much an athlete could earn from the camp and the fees he had to pay if he attended the camp. The rules limited the number of athlete-employees from any one school and prohibited the use of an athlete's name and picture in the camp's publicity or advertising. These rules clearly represented another effort to limit the payments that could result when schools employed student-athletes and also to prevent a coach from using these camps as recruiting tools.

Campus activism in the late 1960s also had an impact on the NCAA. In response to athletes protesting U.S. involvement in the Southeast Asian conflict, the NCAA passed a measure that allowed an institution to take away any financial aid if an athlete was "judged to have been guilty of manifest disobedience through violation of institutional regulations." When asked if coaches would use this rule to get rid of student-athlete troublemakers, Walter Byers, Executive Director of the NCAA said, "That's all hogwash, there are no such coaches."[34]

(In a related incident, the 1969 season marked the 100th anniversary of the first intercollegiate football contest, played between Rutgers and Princeton. Prior to the centennial game, which Rutgers won 29-0, 100 black Princeton students marched clenched-fisted around the field to protest university policies, which, they claimed, collected fees from them but provided no benefits. It was reported that they were booed by the crowd of 31,000.)

In the early 1970s, concern about the rising cost of intercollegiate athletics began to come from many groups besides athletic administrators. Students at the University of Texas took issue with the school's spending $13 million on an addition to the stadium, but only $8 million on new research facilities. At Berkeley, $550,000 spent on a new press box while a faculty hiring freeze was in effect drew student protests. The growing cost of a big-time intercollegiate program, reported as $635,000 in 1960 and $1.322 million in 1969, led many to agree with Boston College's Bill Flynn, head of the NCAA Financial Aid Committee, who said, "If we do not do something about cutting these costs, someone is going to come along and do it for us, someone who does not know athletic problems."[35]

The increased emphasis on cost control led the NCAA to consider, at the 1973 convention, the methods used by members to award financial aid to their student-athletes, producing the first official proposal in 20 years to base athletic grants-in-aid strictly on need. (The idea had been brought up at the 1972 convention, but it did not receive official consideration until the NCAA Council had a year to study it.) This proposal generated considerable debate, and although the membership defeated it, the fact that it reached the floor and forced a vote revealed that Association members did not always agree on difficult financial decisions.

In the 1970s, NCAA members began to encounter severe athletic budgetary pressures from generally spiraling prices and expanding sports programs. Unlike the previous decade, when straightforward cost cutting was rarely discussed in public, NCAA members were now openly searching for ways to reduce expenditures, and one appealing alternative was to reduce the value of the athletic grant-in-aid. But not all agreed that need-based aid was the answer. From the debate prior to the vote, it was clear that division on this issue conformed to expected lines—smaller schools favored the proposal, while the larger schools opposed it.

The question of need-based grants arose again at the 1976 convention, again received serious consideration, and this time nearly passed. After a good deal of parliamentary maneuvering and several votes, the membership took its first-ever roll-call vote and officially defeated the proposal at all three divisions. The closest vote was in Division I, where the supposedly major football schools narrowly defeated the measure, 120-112.

The financial aid issue surfaced once more at the 1977 convention. A dozen financial aid motions were submitted for consideration, but the one that attracted the most attention came out of the University of California, Berkeley. All athletic aid above tuition and mandatory fees, the Berkeley representative proposed, would be based on need. Though this proposal provided schools with more flexibility, it did not gain the support of those with the resources to compete effectively for student-athletes. The proposal also drew criticism from many who predicted that it could not be effectively enforced. Given these objections, the proposal went down to a 142-102 defeat, and all other proposed amendments to the NCAA Constitution on the subject were then withdrawn.

As the 1970s came to a close, the NCAA continued to search for ways to reduce the cost of maintaining athletic programs. In the late 1970s, it adopted several minor rules further restricting payments to student-athletes, but these provided only marginal assistance. The members spoke frequently of resubmitting the need-based grant proposal, but the experience of the mid-1970s discouraged them.

Restricting Economic Competition to Save Members Money

During this period the members of the NCAA also recognized that when one member undertook certain kinds of behavior, all tended to follow. When all members engaged in an activity, none earned an advantage, but all incurred expenses. Thus, all members benefited when certain activities were categorically prohibited by industrywide rules. All the rules detailed in this section, which were rationalized for a variety of reasons, limited competition among the members and, as a result, saved them money.

Among the amendments considered at the 1962 convention, two measures would have limited competition among schools for student-athletes. The first proposed that all student-athletes preregister with the school they planned to attend. Under this "national preregistration plan," a high school athlete would sign an agreement with the school he planned to attend, and all other schools would halt their efforts to recruit him. Further, this plan would have allowed each school to preregister only 35 athletes, of which no more than 25 could be football players.

letter of intent

The anticompetitive features of this preregistration plan were plain even at that time. By agreeing to recognize the validity of a preregistration agreement, all schools would save the resources they otherwise might have spent attempting to attract already committed athletes. The NCAA made little effort to deny this intent.[36]

To ensure that preregistration would work and that schools would honor the agreement, the proposal also included a plan to penalize those athletes who preregistered with one school and then attended another. According to the proposal, an athlete who did this would not be allowed to represent the school he finally attended until he had been in residence two calendar years and could participate for no more than two seasons. Thus, the preregistration proposal contained effective guarantees that it would be honored.

Not all members, however, believed that the policy was worth adopting. The Ivy League schools vocally opposed preregistration because they believed it too closely resembled the contractual agreement between athletes and their professional teams. The members voted to approve the policy, 131 to 98, but they could not reach a two-thirds majority, and the motion failed.

The second major proposal at the 1962 convention with anticompetitive implications focused on the rules by which transfer students became eligible athletes at four-year institutions.[37] This rule required that these students complete one full year (two semesters or three quarters) at the institution before becoming eligible. The NCAA had noticed that several junior college ("juco") students transferred to four-year schools before graduation and just in time to participate on a tournament-bound basketball team. The competition appeal of the rule was obvious: It prevented schools from acquiring superior juco athletes prior to competing in an NCAA tournament. Accordingly, it passed the convention 102 to 36.

Another proposed amendment to the constitution that was based primarily on economic considerations appeared at the 1967 convention. This motion called for the members to limit athletic grants-in-aid to a one-year period, a practice that would give the schools more flexibility with their athletes, since they would not remain committed to an athlete who neither performed adequately nor would relinquish his scholarship. Others thought this policy too arbitrary and too much like a professional contract for amateur sports.

The discussion on this amendment suggested that colleges already enjoyed the option of awarding one-year athletic grants and that this option rendered the motion moot. It was clear, however, that without a binding agreement, schools that awarded longer athletic rides would enjoy an advantage in attracting athletes over the schools that provided aid for shorter periods. The members of the Association voted for this proposal 138 to 109, but since it did not achieve the two-thirds majority, it was not enacted.

Though the cost-cutting measures presented at the annual NCAA conventions had seldom been openly referred to as such, by 1969 the members had become so concerned with the financial pressures on their athletic budgets that they assembled a combined faculty representatives and athletic directors roundtable discussion on "The Rising Cost of Intercollegiate Athletics," a forum that invited members to propose ways to control their production costs.[38] The suggestions included limits on recruiting visits to an athlete's home, limits on an athlete's expense-paid visits to campus, limits on the entertainment a school could provide an athlete, limits on the number of football grants-in-aid, a decrease in the amount of aid awarded student-athletes, an earlier letter of intent signing date to curtail recruiting costs, and limits on the number of full-time coaches.

None of these proposals went beyond the discussion stage in 1969, yet the fact that the Association was openly trying to control its production costs indicates how its goals had changed. Once a group professing concern with only the sporting aspects of higher education, the Association had turned its focus toward the fiscal. By early 1969, only the most naive observer could accept the Association's claims that its actions were motivated by anything but the standard business world desire to increase revenues and decrease costs.

It is also useful to observe how the Association set about organizing the cost-cutting programs. While any institution could unilaterally cut costs by limiting its payments to student-athletes or coaches, most members recognized that no school would voluntarily do this and give the others a competitive advantage at its expense. Instead, the members recognized the importance of making these limits equally incumbent upon everyone. Edwin Cady of Duke University referred directly to the unequal competition that resulted without these limits and the consequent need for standardized rules: "I am for a program whereby we practice economic discipline on a national scale, because nobody has ever been able to keep up with the Joneses."[39]

Among the rules established at the 1969 convention, one prohibited the appearance of a prospective student-athlete on any television show conducted by an NCAA coach and another prohibited athletic staff members from admitting a prospective student-athlete to their sports instructional camp. The first rule prevented coaches from using a television appearance as a recruiting inducement, a television show being a flattering experience for an unschooled adolescent. The coach with his own show, the NCAA reasoned, had an advantage over those who had none.

At its 1970 convention, the Association adopted an important cost-cutting measure covering the purchase of complimentary tickets given to student-athletes. It was and is common practice for a school to provide its student-athletes with complimentary game tickets so that their wives, parents, friends, or relatives can watch them perform. But student-athletes often sold these tickets at opportunistically inflated prices. To stop this form of compensation, the NCAA had allowed the schools to repurchase any unused complimentary tickets at face value. But in 1970, the NCAA put a stop to even this modestly remunerative practice.[40]

The most significant cost-reducing measures of the decade were adopted in August 1975, when the NCAA held only its second special convention, this one dedicated specifically to discussing ways to save money. The most direct step the members took to cut costs was to reduce the number of grants-in-aid that could be offered in football and sports other than football. These additional economy measures caused considerable controversy: a limit on the number of times a coach could visit a recruit (3); limits on the size of a team; limits on the number of coaches on a school's athletic staff; limits on the number of expense-paid visits an athlete could make (6); and limits on the total number of expense-paid visits a school could provide each year (75 in football at the Division I level). Despite the discontent, all measures passed the convention in one vote, but the limit on team size precipitated a lawsuit, which contributed to its abandonment the next year. The limit on the size of the coaching staff also drew a lawsuit, but the Association was sustained in court and the rule stood.[41]

More legislation to control expenditures and limit competition was enacted by the membership at the 1976 annual convention. Among the rules enacted were strict limits on the entertainment provided a recruited athlete and limits on his transportation to and from a college campus (for example, if he came by plane he had to travel tourist class). The NCAA also enacted explicit restrictions on the time of year a recruit could be contacted and the publicity surrounding his signing.

Oddly, the publicity surrounding the signing of a recruit was a unique way to compete for a prospective athlete. On the first legal signing day, coaches would fly around the country to attend signing ceremonies. These ceremonies generally involved flattering publicity for the recruit, his friends, and family. As a result, a university was able to promise a high school athlete that if he signed, the university would provide this type of ceremony.

At Florida, for example, head football coach Doug Dickey once signed a boy on his high school stage in front of the entire school. Appearances by Alabama's football coach Paul "Bear" Bryant on signing day received considerable publicity. The mother of one recruit told this story when Bear came to sign her son Mike:

I made a cake and some sandwiches and things and we had some people in — (three high school coaches, Mike's girlfriend, a television cameraman, some neighbors, two newspaper reporters, a photographer, and a lawyer and Alabama alumnus) — about 25 in all.

Despite an elaborate buffet luncheon, Bryant ate only one apple, and when he left, one of Mike's brothers retrieved the core and showed it off to his friends. "It's the apple that Bear Bryant ate," he boasted.[42]

For the remainder of the 1970s, the Association spent considerable time instituting new limits or tightening old rules that limited the expenses member institutions could incur in recruiting or compensating student-athletes. Among these were rules limiting still further special nonmonetary arrangements that effectively rewarded student-athletes, new limits on the maximum number of grants-in-aid, and further restrictions on the period during which a coach could contact a high school athlete.[43]

By the 1980s, so many rules had been developed by the NCAA that its *Manual*, the source for rules, official interpretations, and case examples, was over 400 pages long.

NOTES

1. H.R. 8757, 87th Cong., 1st sess., 2 (1961), 66.

2. Ibid.

3. *Proceedings of the National Collegiate Athletic Association*, 1963, 203 (hereafter cited as *NCAA Proceedings*).

4. *Rent* is the economics term used here to describe the difference between the competitive price that otherwise would have been paid for broadcast rights and the higher payments the NCAA was able to obtain by restricting the available broadcasts.

5. *Report of the NCAA Television Committee* (Shawnee Mission, Kans.: NCAA, 1965), 38.

6. 1973 *NCAA Proceedings*, 42.

7. Gordon S. White, Jr., "Byers Urges NCAA to Reorganize," *New York Times*, Jan. 13, 1977, 41.

8. Gordon S. White, Jr., "NCAA Gets TV Challenge," *New York Times*, Jan. 8, 1981, sec. 2, 8.

9. 1984-85 *Manual of the NCAA* (Shawnee Mission, Kans.: NCAA, 1984).

10. *Board of Regents of Oklahoma and the University of Georgia Athletic Association v. NCAA*, 546 F. Supp. 1276 (1982) (hereafter cited as *Board of Regents v. NCAA*).

11. Ibid., 1288.

12. Ibid., 1291.

13. Ibid., 1293.

14. Ibid., 1294.

15. Ibid., 1296.
16. Ibid., 1308.
17. Ibid., pp. 1300-1301.
18. *Board of Regents v. NCAA,* 707 F. 2d 1147 (1983).
19. Ibid., 1154.
20. Ibid., 1153.
21. Ibid., 1160.
22. Ibid., 1165.
23. "Justice White Gets Top NCAA Prize in Coast Ceremony," *New York Times,* Jan. 8, 1969, 57.
24. *Board of Regents v. NCAA,* 104 S. Ct. 2948 (1984).
25. Ibid., 2961.
26. Ibid., 2963-64.
27. Ibid., 2968-69.
28. Ibid., 2970.
29. See 1967 *NCAA Proceedings,* 86.
30. See 1962 *NCAA Proceedings,* 128-29.
31. See 1963 *NCAA Proceedings,* 147.
32. See 1962 *NCAA Proceedings,* 152.
33. "Three College Coaches Label Pro Football Draft Unfair," *New York Times,* July 29, 1958, 27.
34. Gordon S. White Jr., "College Athletes Who Protest To Face Loss of Financial Aid," *New York Times,* Jan. 9, 1969, 24.
35. Leonard Koppett, "Colleges Question Old View On Sports," *New York Times,* Jan. 11, 1971, 70.
36. See 1962 *NCAA Proceedings,* 258.
37. See 1962 *NCAA Proceedings,* 282-84.
38. See 1969 *NCAA Proceedings,* 36-49.
39. 1969 *NCAA Proceedings,* 48.
40. See 1970 *NCAA Proceedings,* a-22.
41. See *Lawrence H. Hennessey and Wendel Hudson v. NCAA,* 564 F. 2d 1136 (1977).
42. "Sports Recruiting: For Every Winner, A Hundred Losers," *New York Times,* March 13, 1974, 46.
43. See 1978 *NCAA Proceedings,* Appendix A, and 1979 *NCAA Proceedings,* Appendix A.

CHAPTER 5

Operating the Intercollegiate Athletic Cartel

Americans object to cartels because they restrict production and raise prices. The increased prices draw public ire, but the real problem results as the higher prices thwart the efficiencies of the market system because people who might otherwise have made a purchase cannot. In economics jargon, the difference between the higher, manipulated price and the lower price that a free market would generate is referred to as *rents.* In a cartel, producers are said to *capture* these rents from the consumer, or stated more colloquially, cartels "exploit the consumer."

Less frequently, members of a cartel band together to restrict payment to the factors used in the production process. In this instance, a cartel is said to capture rents by paying a lower price to a factor (for example, labor or an essential raw material) than it otherwise would have commanded in a free market. In popular slang, these cartels "exploit the worker."

Traditionally, cartel analysis has focused on the restrictions in the output market. It should be clear, however, that a cartel could be particularly profitable if it could capture rents on the input side as well as the rents from the output market. We can find few examples of such a cartel, but the National Collegiate Athletic Association (NCAA) is one.   *capturing rents on the input side*

TRANSFERRING MONEY TO ATHLETIC DEPARTMENTS

As we have seen, the rules and regulations adopted by the NCAA influence that market in which student-athletes exchange their skills for grants-in-aid. Uninhibited exchange between student-athletes and universities would exist were it not for the fact that the NCAA disrupts this free exchange with its lengthy list detailing what compensation a university can and cannot provide a student-athlete for his service. The compensation the NCAA does allow, moreover, falls well below what a skilled athlete could command in a free market. Thus, the NCAA's intervention has had the same effect on the student-athlete market as any other price control set below the equilibrium price.

The members of the NCAA save the money they would have otherwise paid to student-athletes by establishing a standard price for their services and then enforcing that agreement. With the NCAA controlling a student-athlete's wages, the producers of the games retain the surplus over the amount the NCAA allows for inducing athletes to attend a particular university. With this restrictive policy in place, and provided no unsanctioned competition for student-athletes occurs (an important proviso), producers can capture rents from (exploit) the truly skilled athletes.

The NCAA has also established rules that restrict the behavior of its members in the output market of athletic contests. Without NCAA rules limiting the number of athletic contests, colleges might stage more athletic competition, with the effect of lowering ticket and broadcast prices. But NCAA rules limit the number of games played, and consequently, the institutions cannot engage in this sort of free economic competition.

These restrictions on production increase the amount of money schools earn from playing the game, and they provide NCAA schools with larger payments than they would have received had they played more games. Thus, one effect of the NCAA's intervention in the output market is to allow its schools to secure rents from demanders (exploit the customers or paying public).

Given this understanding of how NCAA policies allow its members to capture rents in both the input and output markets, one can better understand why the producers have banded together to adopt these policies. In a standard business setting such rents as these are normally divided among the producers so as to maximize wealth. But partly because of their institutional settings, the producers of college athletic contests cannot do this. Consequently, what the producers do with the money they retain by paying athletes less than their fair-market wage and by charging customers a higher than fair-market admission price merits some examination.

The NCAA is an unincorporated, "nonprofit" organization that works closely with the athletic departments of its 793 member colleges and universities. A college athletic department producing athletic contests behaves much like any other business firm producing a product, except for these two differences: First, while a business firm seeks to maximize profits, there is some question about the objectives of an athletic department. Second, an athletic department has no monitor or residual claimant.

A business firm hires and buys men and material and sells goods and services in an effort to maximize profits, where profit equals revenue less cost. In such a firm there exists a monitor to oversee the employees and ensure that they carry out their responsibilities. The monitor meters employee performance and minimizes production costs. His incentive is his share of what remains after all contractual obligations have been met. If he does his job well, that residual and his reward will be large. If he has failed, his reward will be commensurately low. Theoretically, his monitoring activity ensures production.

While a few athletic departments may eagerly attempt to maximize their profits, this is not the objective of the majority. One finds, however, a plausible explanation for the behavior of NCAA athletic departments in Armen Alchian's definition of a *restricted profit rate firm*. This type of firm faces institutional constraints that limit the profit it can earn and accordingly alters the behavior of the management. When it reaches its profit limit, the cost of certain kinds of behavior lessens. This specific behavior may feature a transition from wealth maximization to utility maximization. Here is how Alchian describes this transition:

[T]he manager's behavior is [now] interpreted as choosing among opportunities to obtain increments of nonpecuniary goods in his utility function (e.g., pretty secretaries, thick rugs, friendly colleagues, a leisurely work load, executive washrooms, a larger work staff).[1]

An NCAA athletic department faces two constraints that make it behave like a profit-restricted firm. The first is inherent in the institutional setting itself. A university generally operates in a nonprofit atmosphere and, although the production of athletic contests devolves to the athletic department, many of the same contractual arrangements that exist between the university and its employees also exist between the athletic department and its employees. Thus, no monitor or residual claimant exists in the athletic department.

The person with responsibilities that most resemble the monitor's is the athletic director or "AD." In contrast to a traditional business setting, where senior management is compensated for performance, an AD usually receives a salary and does not have as strong an incentive to monitor as carefully as those in business. This doesn't mean that the AD altogether lacks incentives: A superior performance must be rewarded, or he may seek another job. But because an AD may have to wait awhile for his contract to expire, the incentives he faces do not produce the efficiencies of the arrangement between a traditional firm and its monitor.

The second constraint on an athletic department comes from the academic environment around it. Members of the college community occasionally view athletics as a threatening force that dominates rather than complements university life. These individuals tend to deplore what appears to be a double academic standard for athletes and athletic administrators. Additional tension arises from the fact that athletic departments operate as independent financial entities. The large athletic profits contribute to an antiathletic mood in a faculty theoretically capable of appropriating some of those resources. This is one reason for the limit, or the appearance of a limit, on athletic profitability.

Since the athletic department assigns no monitor to take home the residuals and since it faces inherent pressure to avoid unseemly profits, one can expect of it certain kinds of behavior. For example, while the business firm has a monitor or residual claimant to minimize costs, the absence of such a person in an athletic department should lead to inflated athletic expenditures on such items as salaries, scholarships, recruiting, traveling, equipment, facilities, and office expenses.

Still, an athletic department does have some incentive to increase the revenue from the sale of its product (that is, to maximize its budget). Larger revenues mean more teams, athletes, and coaches and higher salaries. Thus, this analysis suggests that athletic expenditures should increase up to the level of the athletic revenue. This cost-increasing process, traced directly to the lack of monitoring, may explain the numerous complaints from athletic departments about the difficulties of keeping costs below revenue.

According to a 1977 NCAA-financed survey, the members who maintained programs fielding teams in ten or more sports (including big-time football) earned average total revenues of $2.183 million, but had total expenses that averaged $2.213 million.[2] Thus, in 1977, the members of the NCAA that responded to this survey ran an average deficit of $30,000. Many of the schools attributed this rapid increase in expenses to the effects of inflation; yet as the survey pointed out, the general price index between 1970 and 1977 increased by approximately 54 percent, while the surveyed expenses had increased by 75 percent. All this suggests that the difference actually reflects the acquisition of nonpecuniary benefits by the athletic departments. Some crude evidentiary support for this suggestion comes from the same survey, which reported that the percentage of total expenditures on grants-in-aid and salaries and wages had decreased between 1969 and 1977, while the percentage of total expenditures on team and other travel, equipment and supplies, and all other expenses had increased.[3]

An updated 1982 version of the same survey showed a similar pattern in these miscellaneous expenditures. There it was reported by the Division I-A and I-AA football schools that expenses unrelated to specific sports—such items as maintenance expenses, utilities, program administration, office supplies, certain salaries, and communication expenses—had grown from 27 percent of total athletic expenditures in 1977 to 33 percent of total expenditures reported in 1981.[4]

In view of the NCAA policies that allow its members to capture rents fore and aft, as it were, one explanation of where these resources go must focus on the institutional setting. Because members of the athletic department cannot simply pocket their profits and, therefore, tend to maximize their own wealth, one expects them to acquire fancy offices and bigger and better facilities, at least in comparison with the rest of the campus. Thus inclined to maximize utility by acquiring nonpecuniary benefits, no athletic department members would be particularly eager to return money to the university. Any such money that finds its way to the institution's general fund usually serves to calm the naturally troubled waters between athletics and academics. This money purchases goodwill, which is itself a nonpecuniary benefit.

Again, support for this general unwillingness to return money to the university comes from the 1982 survey. When asked to indicate the financial objectives of the athletic program, only 1 percent in 1981 (and only 4 percent in 1977) of the Division I football schools responded by indicating they sought to earn profits to support nonathletic activities of the institution.[5]

Another explanation for those NCAA policies that restrict payments to athletes has to do with the problem of cross-sport subsidization. The money saved by restricting certain behavior in the major revenue-generating sports can theoretically help finance other sports that generate insufficient funds to cover their production costs. Hence, the heavy regulation of football that makes it more profitable than it otherwise might be tends to produce at least some extra money to finance the minor sports. (Conversely, when the revenue from football and basketball declines, a likely first move is to cut the nonrevenue sports.)

According to the studies cited earlier, the average major college football program produced a profit of $288,000 in 1977 and $584,000 in 1981.[6] A large portion of this money no doubt remained in the athletic department's general fund to support at least some unprofitable sports. Consequently, one effect of restricting payments to college football players and limiting games in order to raise ticket prices is to earn rents often used to finance other intercollegiate sports. Based on the fact that no sport is as profitable as football and the NCAA frequently points out that more than one million student-athletes compete in the sports it sanctions, it is clear that this transfer must be significant.

CARTEL COMPOSITION, DECISION MAKING, AND THE NCAA

Because a cartel must consist of two or more producers, most of its behavior reflects collective decision making. This collective decision making invariably exercises certain influences. For example, the cost of making collective decisions increases as the group grows. One way to minimize the cost and confusion that result when large groups make collective decisions is to ensure that all the firms share approximately the same objective and cost functions so that each decision has approximately the same impact on all members. Consequently, a cartel composed of producers with similar goals and methods will find it less cumbersome to make collective decisions than a smaller group composed of members with diverse interests.

This need for shared similar goals and methods cannot be overemphasized in view of the strong incentives to cheat on any limiting agreement. Because any firm can gain an advantage in the cartel by deviating from the restrictive agreement and because all firms recognize this fact, cartels tend to be unstable. As Charles M. Schwab once remarked, "Many of them lasted a day, some of them lasted until the gentlemen could go to the telephone from the room in which they were made."[7]

Collective decision making also affects the incentives of the cartelized firms. If a firm outside the cartel chooses to take more risks in pursuit of profit, it alone incurs whatever losses or enjoys whatever gains come its way. But in a cartel, any advantageous discovery must be shared. Under cartel rules, a firm cannot expand production and reap the increased profits its discovery promises. Hence, collective action discourages the firms in a cartel from developing new projects or processes.

Collective decision making in a cartel also exerts an important influence on the distribution of the rents the members generate. If decisions come by way of a voting rule that gives each member equal say and if the gains from cartel membership accrue equally, the potential for problems associated with the redistribution of income among members is small. It is also small, even though the cartel rents may accrue unequally, if the voting rule allows the votes of the members to be weighted according to the magnitude of their wealth. Under these circumstances, members have little incentive or chance to redistribute wealth.

The largest potential for income redistribution problems within a cartel occurs when the gains from membership accrue unequally but all the members enjoy the same voting privileges. Under such circumstances, a minority of the membership could conceivably collect a majority of the rents while the majority of members outvote the lucrative minority and (again, theoretically) transfer revenue from the wealthier group to itself.

A voting rule like this threatens the viability of any cartel because the "have" firms may prefer to withdraw and compete against the "have-not" firms. In fact, they will almost certainly do so unless they encounter a sufficiently large penalty for withdrawal. In such a situation, the "have" firms generally attempt to impose a decision-making rule that allows them to defeat those proposals that would redistribute their income.

Equipped with this general discussion of the composition of a cartel and the implications of its collective decision making, we can observe how major problems confronting the NCAA have been related to the difficulties of collective behavior on such a large scale.

Initially the NCAA consisted of 62 institutions, most of them located in the northeastern United States. Because football was often a college's only athletic team, the early NCAA members maintained modest and similar athletic programs. As a result, few major disagreements arose within the NCAA during its early years.

To make its decisions, the NCAA chose the one-school, one-vote rule and also gave athletic conferences one vote. To amend the NCAA constitution, a motion had to receive a two-thirds majority while only a simple majority was needed to amend the bylaws. With a homogeneous membership, this voting rule served well until shortly after World War II.

After World War II, however, the NCAA, whose membership had grown steadily since 1905, turned to controlling the televising of college football. The NCAA's decision to restrict all live broadcasts led to the first major disagreement between NCAA members and provides an apt example of the problems collective decision making generates. Those schools that maintained highly competitive football teams (most prominently the Universities of Pennsylvania and Notre Dame) resisted limits on their television appearances and revenues. The majority of schools, which rarely appeared on television and saw their gate receipts eroded by television broadcasts, preferred a policy of restrictive broadcasting. Under the one-school, one-vote rule, the majority imposed its will on the minority and transferred the television money to itself.

As the Association grew, its members increasingly differed in the size of their athletic programs, their athletic philosophies, and their approaches to athletic problems. Schools with larger budgets openly sought national championships; others had smaller budgets and more modest aspirations. To solve some of the conflict inherent in these differences, the NCAA divided its membership into university and college divisions for the purposes of both athletic competition and common problem solving at the conventions. The Association did not, however, go all the way with this solution, and most decisions were made en masse at this time. ~~Division IA I-AA, II, III~~

As the NCAA entered the 1970s, tight budgets began to exacerbate the other problems just described. But as soon as the schools with large athletic problems offered solutions to these problems (such as forming a separate group composed of only those committed to big-time programs), they were rejected by the smaller schools. The solutions presented by the smaller schools (for example, need-based aid) were, in turn, rejected by the larger schools. Thus by the early 1970s, the differences between NCAA members had begun to strain the structure of the cartel.

Meanwhile, the larger schools began to grumble over the number of appearances their football teams made on television. Under NCAA policy, the only way to receive a share of the television rents was to play on television. The larger schools with the larger number of fans claimed that the smaller schools too often preempted them. The schools with strong football programs recognized that, freed from the NCAA's restrictive policy, they could increase their television earnings. Hints of an independent football association began to surface.

To address these problems, the NCAA reorganized its membership in 1973 into three categories (Divisions I, II, and III) based on the size, scheduling, and commitment to the business aspects of the sport. This reorganization appeared to remedy most of the problems that had necessitated the special summer convention—until, that is, it developed that Division I contained schools that simply could not reach the big-time level consistently. The schools with highly competitive programs immediately called for an additional reorganization of Division I, but their demands went unheeded for five years.

The most blatant attempt to use the NCAA to redistribute money came when the so-called Robin Hood proposals reached the 1976 NCAA annual convention. Under these proposals, income would have been redistributed from the big-time, frequently televised, bowl-dominating schools to those schools with smaller programs and little television exposure. These proposals were voted down in part because the major sports schools that stood to lose threatened to withdraw from the NCAA. Yet the proposals demonstrated that, as long as the schools with a smaller commitment to sports had the same voice as the larger schools with multimillion-dollar sports programs and these less committed schools comprised the majority, the ideal circumstances for redistributing income were present.

The schools committed to maintaining major sports programs became increasingly frustrated with the NCAA and formed the CFA in 1977 to discuss problems and develop solutions. One prominent idea they lobbied for was the removal of smaller schools from the NCAA's Division I. In 1978, Division I was reorganized into Divisions I-A and I-AA. The College Football Association members had envisioned Division I-A as consisting of only the big-time athletic schools, which numbered 81, including all of the 61 CFA members plus the members of the Big Ten and Pac 10 conferences. But under the Ivy League amendment, any school that maintained 12 or more intercollegiate sports could join Division I-A, and more than 56 of them did. This amendment increased the size of Division I-A to 137 and prevented the 61 CFA members from controlling the rules by which they agreed to operate.

The members of the CFA were still discontented with the way decisions were made, and they attempted to sign their own television contract with NBC in mid-1981. The NCAA reorganized Division I-A along the lines of the CFA's earlier requests in December of 1981, but by then, it was too late for the NCAA to appease the CFA because its members had instituted legal action that would ultimately determine that the schools, not the NCAA, owned the television broadcast rights.

The breakdown of the NCAA's control of college football television highlights the significance of organizing a successful decision-making mechanism in a cartel. While NCAA rules encouraged redistribution, schools recognizing this early, like Notre Dame and Pennsylvania, were unable to oppose the whole Association. Eventually, however, the CFA, with a sufficiently large and influential membership to form a creditable competing sports organization, demonstrated that the method by which the NCAA made decisions to divide the rents from television was unworkable.

MONITORING IN THE INTERCOLLEGIATE CARTEL

As we have seen, the NCAA maintains its efficient cartel by restricting behavior in the output and input markets of college athletics. In the output market, NCAA regulations restrict the number of athletic contests produced by member institutions, and when the NCAA negotiated the television contract, the NCAA Television Committee carefully directed the televising of these contests. The Association, however, spends few resources monitoring the output market. Because of the unique nature of the product, no unsanctioned contest could go unnoticed. Furthermore, the way the Television Committee coordinated with the contracting network (they agreed on the teams to be televised and the areas to receive the telecasts) and the large number of viewers televised games attract prevented any college team from appearing on television without the NCAA's knowledge and ensured that the NCAA could inexpensively enforce its rules restricting behavior of the output market.

In the input market, the NCAA restricts the payments to student-athletes and in general controls the conduct of both recruiting coaches and recruited athletes. Because the recruiting and maintenance of student-athletes is, however, far more private than behavior in the output market, NCAA rule violations tend to occur more frequently in the input market, and as a result, the NCAA deploys most of its monitoring resources there.

Given this outline of the NCAA's monitoring priorities, one can analyze the process by which student-athletes exchange their services for so-called scholarships, explore the ways in which educational institutions compete for student-athletes, and detail the ways in which the NCAA restrains this competition.

Cartel Monitoring and NCAA Efforts

A critical issue in cartel theory is chiseling—critical because cheating on limiting agreements threatens the life of the cartel. Understanding the threat, most cartels establish some sort of monitoring mechanism to prevent chiseling.

The ideal cartel monitoring arrangement allows a monitor to count output by hand and ensure, by observing each transaction, that the members charge the predetermined price. The practical impossibility of this ideal situation reduces cartel monitoring to a choice of monitoring either price or output.

Stating prices publicly in no way ensures their accuracy. Tie-in sales and kickback arrangements are just two ways output can be expanded without changing the posted price. Thus, the fact that a monitor knows his prices does not guarantee a stable cartel agreement.

Knowledge of the quantity a member of the cartel is producing is much more important. This is because price (and also whether the member is cheating on the cartel agreement) can be determined if quantity is known. Furthermore, compared to price, which may never be known, output tends to be countable. One would only have to sit in a Mideast seaport and observe the number of loaded, outbound oil tankers to get a good idea of how much oil a country exports. Other things being equal, the cartel monitor tends to be more concerned with output than price.

The next point to consider is where output monitoring takes place — at the point of production or at the point of sale. One would expect it to occur where the observing was easiest — that is to say, where monitoring costs are lowest. If costs increase with size, monitoring should take place where the smallest group is involved.

If there are fewer producers than consumers, output should be monitored at the point of production, as with lawyers, doctors, and dentists. Output is controlled by restricting entry into these professions (the point of production); hence we see limits on the number of medical and law schools and the emergence of professional qualifying examinations. Such raw materials as oil would also fall into this category of monitoring at the point of production.

If, however, there are too many producers, it would be logical to monitor output at the point of sale. The expansive geographical regions over which farming and ranching take place in the United States make it expensive to visit each location to observe how much of each crop or animal is being produced. Instead, it would be less expensive to control output if a central market existed where crops or animals are sold. Agricultural products provide an example of goods that could be monitored at the point of sale, with farm trade associations as one group that might do the monitoring.

Turning now to college athletics, where output is athletic contests, we find fewer producers here than purchasers. But in terms of cartel monitoring, the NCAA finds the point of production and the point of sale of athletic contests in precisely the same place. Hence, the output monitoring location is obvious: it is the campus.

The NCAA's effort to monitor college athletics is also facilitated by the fact that a public record of the outcome of the contests is sure to appear in the media. The production of an unmonitored unit of output would, therefore, be impossible. Consequently, the NCAA can cheaply and easily monitor the output in the sports for which it limits the number of contests. (In Division I, for example, the NCAA has specified contest limits for baseball, basketball, football, ice hockey, soccer, and softball.)

In the input market, the Association's experiences in the first half of the twentieth century revealed that unrestrainted competition encourages athletic departments and alumni associations to offer student-athletes direct monetary payments and such inducements as cars and clothing. But ineffective rules and voluntary compliance demonstrated that limiting agreements had to be enforced. Thus, the NCAA set up an enforcement mechanism to prevent cheating on the rules that limited competition and saved its member schools money.

Without such a mechanism, schools in search of highly skilled student-athletes had an incentive to make unsanctioned payments. If a recruited athlete helped produce a successful, attractive, profitable, winning team, more people would attend the games. This increase in demand would lead to higher admission prices, more television appearances, and greater revenue for the school. Superior athletes also decreased the cost of producing athletic contests. A team of highly skilled student-athletes requires less training time and lessens the pressure on the athletic staff, the equipment and facilities, and the athletic department budget.

To prevent this destructive competition, to limit an athlete's wages, and to increase thereby the rents accruing to athletic departments, the NCAA established a series of committees designed to monitor its rules. Those committees evolved into what is known today as the Committee on Infractions, which works closely with the Association's Compliance and Enforcement Department. (This is one of six NCAA departments—the others being administration, championships, communications, legislative services, and publishing.) The 15 members of Compliance and Enforcement conduct the actual investigations of NCAA members, but in 1982 the NCAA signed a contract with a private investigative firm, National Fire Associates of Kansas City, which put an additional 40 part-time detectives at its disposal.

An investigation into a possible violation begins with an allegation or complaint by an individual over a failure to comply with NCAA regulations or at the initiative of the enforcement staff. This staff, according to the NCAA's rules, must investigate the allegation(s) and present its findings to the Committee on Infractions. If the assistant executive director for enforcement decides that the violation was isolated or inadvertent, or one that produced a limited recruiting advantage for the violator (these are called secondary violations), he may force the university to forfeit the games involving the athlete in question, order the university to stop pursuing a recruit, prohibit the coaching staff from recruiting for one year, fine the school, or cut the number of grants-in-aid the university may award.

If he decides that the violation was not of the secondary type, the Committee on Infractions listens to the entire report of the investigative staff. If the Committee on Infractions determines that the violation is minor, it may reprimand or censure the university without a hearing. If the committee considers the violation serious, it opens an official inquiry (subject to a multitude of NCAA rules and regulations) and invites the university to respond to the charge(s) at a hearing. The committee then weighs the evidence, and if it decides to punish the institution, it chooses from among a variety of penalties that include probation for a year or more, ineligibility for NCAA events or television programs it administers, or prohibition against recruiting athletes, awarding grants-in-aid, or even participating in the sport in question.

In addition, the NCAA has also stipulated that members who violate Association rules within five years of the starting date of a major penalty be declared repeat violators. Repeat violators are automatically subject to minimum penalties, which could include prohibition from participating or recruiting in the sport for up to two years, removal of NCAA officials representing the school, or the forfeit of NCAA voting privileges for four years.[8] The severity of these penalties for the repeat offender has led many to nickname this section of the NCAA rulebook the Death Penalty.

An institution has the right to appeal the decision of the Committee on Infractions to the 46-member Council of the NCAA.

Monitoring Recruiting

Monitoring recruiting activity presents the biggest challenge to the NCAA because of the many coaches, athletes, administrators, and alumni involved. Recruiting generally begins when, having displayed the requisite skills in high school competition, an athlete is contacted by those universities seeking his services. While a superior athlete may receive contacts from hundreds of schools, a few universities with established reputations contact only those athletes who contact them first. In the highly competitive recruiting arena, however, these schools are few.

A close analogy to this process occurs in U.S. professional baseball where players not under contract after six years in the league become free agents, able to search the market and sign a contract with the team of their choice.[9] As the baseball player searches the market, information about the value of his skills emerges from the bid each team makes for his services. Important adjustments in the bidding process take place as the player or his agent informs each team of other offers. When the player and a team finally reach an agreement, they sign a contract. The market provides an efficient outcome, and the team that is willing to make the best offer wins the player's services.

The market situation for student-athletes bears many similarities to the professional baseball player market, but it also has several important differences. Like the baseball player who searches for the team best for him (the one offering a larger salary, a chance to contend for the pennant, or an attractive location), the student-athlete searches for the right university for him. While a university may offer a student-athlete many things (like the chance to "start," a new dorm with private rooms, or the opportunity to study under the most distinguished economics faculty in the country), one of the things a university cannot do is offer him money for his services. Because NCAA rules limit the amount that a player may receive for his services, the competitive bidding process that takes place in a free market does not exist in the college athletic market.

The free agent professional athlete can determine his value by the offers teams make for his services. As teams bid for those services, the interest decreases as the offers escalate, until eventually the bidder with the most attractive offer wins. Because this procedure is absent in college athletics, the exact value of an athlete's service is more difficult to determine. As a proxy he may base the demand for his services on the number of schools that write, call, or visit him, but this method is not as reliable as the pricing mechanism.

In fact, without a pricing mechanism based on cost-benefit information, schools have an incentive to pursue the athlete longer than they otherwise might. Thus, the contracting process between athlete and university tends to drag on at length, involving more universities for a longer time than if the process had a price mechanism to allocate resources.

The final agreement between an athlete and a school closely resembles the formal agreement between an athlete and his professional team. Once a professional athlete has signed a contract, any attempt by another team to induce him to violate his contract will bring charges of tampering, a transgression punishable by monetary sanctions or by the withdrawal of such league privileges as a choice in the draft. When a senior high school athlete decides which university to attend, he often signs a national letter of intent that binds him to that university.

The national letter of intent is a one-page statement signed by an athlete, his parents, and the athletic director, advising all readers that the athlete agrees to attend Bigtime U. Henceforth all subscribers to the national of letter of intent agreement cease recruiting that athlete. In return, the agreement calls for penalties on any athlete who signs an agreement with one school and then attends another. There are, of course, exceptions to this last rule, but these apply to obvious situations — for example, an athlete not meeting the entrance requirements.

While most universities honor the national letter of intent in their dealings with the high school athlete, the market for athletes transferring from junior colleges to four-year institutions (the so-called juco transfers) remains hotly competitive because no letter of intent applies to these athletes. Two-year junior colleges amount to a lively feeder system for major four-year universities, providing a steady supply of athletes who were unable to move directly from high school to the larger schools.[10] At the end of their two years, provided they have the requisite grade point average and enough credits (again, this is not a universal requirement), these athletes can transfer to a four-year university and participate in sports. Because junior college athletes have already proven their competitive skills against college athletes, juco transfers attract a lot of recruiting attention. Also, unlike an athlete who transfers from one four-year institution to another and must, therefore, sit out a year, a juco transfer can compete immediately.

The market for superior junior college athletes has become so competitive in recent years that in addition to the usual "baby-sitting" practices to ensure that no other university steals a recruit, assistant coaches often walk a juco transfer to his first class to establish, in conformity with NCAA rules, that he is officially enrolled and thereby make it possible for him to leave without sitting out a whole year.

The complicated and unpredictable nature of recruiting allows one to focus on no central location, per se, where student-athletes' services are exchanged. Recruiting can take place almost anywhere, and, as a result, ensuring that it all proceeds according to the rules can be extremely difficult. Nevertheless, the overall recruiting process does suggest a monitoring method.

When the athlete compares universities, he compares the offers each has made, and as he compares, the flow of information between him and the various schools increases the likelihood that one school will learn what the other is offering. In short, news of a prohibited offer tends to be transmitted from the supplier (a student-athlete) to the demander (the universities), a fact that largely explains the NCAA's current monitoring policy. Consequently, the NCAA relies on the information conveyed between a recruit and the schools recruiting him and the incentive each school has to eliminate the other in the competition for a recruit, and it accepts all allegations of possible violations from any source and investigates the reasonably substantiated charges.

The NCAA itself describes the procedure this way:

All allegations and complaints relative to . . . the member's violation of the legislation or regulations of the Association . . . shall be received by the committee or the Association's executive director and channeled to the NCAA investigative staff.[11]

Thus, in situations where monitoring all incidents would be prohibitively expensive, efficient monitoring consists of encouraging competitors to report violations as they see them and investigating a likely selection of incidents.

The nature of its product also gives the NCAA one monitoring advantage. At the end of each high school season, various national and local sports organizations and publications compile lists of the country's top players (for example, *Parade* magazine's list of high school all-Americans and the various district all-stars). With this very public information listing the country's superior high school athletes, the NCAA can concentrate on monitoring a relatively small group. So far, this monitoring has included actual visits from the enforcement staff, mailed notices detailing what a college coach is allowed to offer, and postrecruiting questionnaires and debriefings.

Punishing and Rewarding Member Institutions

The NCAA's policy of allowing anyone to report rule violations raises the question: Why should a school report violations? Without attractive rewards for the informer or unpleasant costs for remaining silent, one would not normally expect violations to be brought reliably to the NCAA's attention. The NCAA does not reward its informants directly. Instead, they receive an indirect reward by seeing a rival university penalized. Sometimes this reward is not so indirect (if, for example, the penalty keeps a rival out of postseason competition and the informant goes in its place). For a direct rival school, the cost of silence is having to compete against the illegally recruited athlete. Nationwide recruiting has reduced this probability; however, since a university competes against more schools across a wider area in basketball than in any other sport, numerous allegations arise out of basketball, mainly because the chance of competing against an improperly recruited athlete is so much greater.

If the NCAA seeks to discourage cheating, it must also be able to impose the penalties appropriate under the circumstances. If, for example, the rewards of cheating exceed the penalties, it makes sense to violate the rules. This is what North Carolina State University learned from the David Thompson affair. In 1972, the NCAA found N. C. State guilty of violating its rules when it recruited Thompson for basketball in 1970. Given a one-year probation and denied television appearances and postseason competition for the 1972-73 season, the Wolfpack basketball team, led by Thompson, went on to win the NCAA basketball championship the very next year, receiving monetary rewards far in excess of the earlier penalty. Obviously, if the NCAA seeks to discourage this kind of calculated cheating, it must ensure that the penalties it imposes outweigh the advantages a chiseler counts on.

The key to controlling violators is to keep the penalties high, and the penalties the NCAA is empowered to use are quite stiff. They include

[T]ermination of the coaching contract of the head coach and any assistants involved; suspension or termination of the employment status of any other institutional employee who may be involved; severance of relations with any representative of the institution's athletics interests who may be involved; the debarment of the head or assistant coach from any coaching, recruiting or speaking engagements for a specified period, and the prohibition of all recruiting in a specified sport for a specified period.[12]

But seldom, if ever, does the NCAA impose these penalties. The case of Jerry Tarkanian best highlights this point.

Jerry Tarkanian was the basketball coach for California State University, Long Beach. Shortly after he transformed the Cal-Long Beach basketball team into a national power, Tarkanian left Long Beach to coach at the University of Nevada, Las Vegas (UNLV). A subsequent NCAA investigation revealed that Tarkanian had committed many violations during his tenure at Long Beach. In 1974, the NCAA put Long Beach, and its new basketball coach, Lute Olsen, on probation while Tarkanian, who had committed the violations, escaped unsanctioned.

The NCAA went on to investigate Tarkanian's methods at Las Vegas, and found that he had continued to commit NCAA rule violations by providing excessive aid to athletes, cosigning auto loans, and providing unauthorized air transportation while building the Running Rebel basketball program. In the fall of 1977, the NCAA severely sanctioned UNLV and ordered it to suspend the coach for two years. In September 1977 President Donald H. Baepler suspended Tarkanian. But Tarkanian quickly obtained a restraining order from Judge James Brennan of the Nevada State District Court, and after a hearing, a permanent injunction was issued barring the University from suspending him. In October, a spokesman for the University said it would appeal the decision but acknowledged that it would take one year before the case got to court. Known in the college basketball business as Tark the Shark, Tarkanian quickly returned to courtside where his athletes imported from distant cities achieved high winning percentages. (In 1984 the case was finally settled, long after the sanction had expired, when the Nevada Supreme Court made the injunction blocking the suspension permanent.)

The Tarkanian case illustrates the NCAA's inability to punish individual rule breakers. Jerry Tarkanian, a consistent violator, proved that the NCAA was unable to issue a punishment that would countermand his rights under the law. Thus, whle the NCAA has set up a system of penalties, it seems unable to punish individual violators.

Because the NCAA has no legal power to fire or imprison a coach or student who violates its rules, it really has less direct control over certain kinds of behavior than it needs to maintain the stability of its cartel. Instead of punishing violators itself, the NCAA tries to force the school to penalize the athlete or coach. In this way, it makes the universities responsible for their behavior. Theoretically, the threat of a penalty encourages a school to monitor its own athletic department, and it licenses the NCAA to impose larger penalties since it finds it easier to proceed against the school than an individual.

In its constitution the NCAA specifically points out that the institution is responsible for its athletic program and for such independent organizations as alumni associations engaged in athletic-related activities such as recruiting. The Association's constitutional bylaws make it clear that the school's responsiblity for its athletic department and associated groups like alumni and booster clubs must include carefully watching how they spend their money. For example, according to NCAA rules:

A staff member of the institution periodically shall inspect the financial records of the alumni organization and certify that the expenditures comply with the rules and regulations of the NCAA.[18]

The NCAA's rule requiring that the universities themselves determine eligibility has frequently come under attack. Many feel that because the NCAA makes the rules and can conduct investigations, it should declare whether or not student-athletes are eligible. The NCAA, however, has decided that such a system would engender a catch-me-if-you-can attitude among its members, with the NCAA's enforcement forces hopelessly outmanned. The Association is correct:

The probability of catching violators would fall drastically (only one small group would be policing the cartel agreements instead of the entire staff and membership). By making the institutions responsible, the NCAA can impose much larger and, theoretically, prohibitive costs on violators.

But the members are not helpless before the NCAA's policing. They can purchase some insurance by joining other schools and forming a conference, a group of schools with athletic programs of roughly the same caliber located in the same general region. They usually agree to compete primarily with each other, and they often strike revenue-sharing agreements. For example, each team may devote a percentage of the money it earns from a television appearance to a kitty divided among all members. With this risk-averse strategy, teams protect themselves against the possibility of a lackluster season without a television appearance and, therefore, no television revenue. By joining a conference, a school also lowers the cost of violating NCAA rules.

Two of the most costly penalties the NCAA imposes are (1) restriction on television appearances, and (2) restrictions on postseason competition. These penalties can, and have, cost universities large amounts of money, making a discovered violation painfully expensive. But if the institution joins a conference that pools television revenue, it will collect a share of another school's television and bowl appearances and, in effect, lower the cost of its violation.

From this tendency to form conferences and share revenue, one can draw certain inferences. First, football (and basketball) continue to generate the most revenue, and as the penalties for violating NCAA rules increase, one would expect more conferences to form in order to lower the cost of these violations. Second, the risk-averse nature of conferences and their ability to reduce the effect of NCAA penalties would lead one to expect proportionally more rule violations from conference schools than independent schools. Thus, while the NCAA has instituted an efficient system to monitor a larger group by increasing both the probabilities of being caught and the cost of violating the rules, universities have found ways to reduce these costs by forming risk-sharing associations called conferences.

NOTES

1. Armen Alchian, "The Basis of Some Recent Advances in the Theory of the Firm," *Journal of Industrial Economics*, Nov. 1965, 34.

2. Mitchell H. Raiborn, *Revenue and Expenses of Intercollegiate Athletic Programs* (Shawnee Mission, Kans.: NCAA, 1977), 39.

3. Ibid., 25.

4. Mitchell H. Raiborn, *Revenue and Expenses of Intercollegiate Athletic Programs* (Shawnee Mission, Kans.: NCAA, 1982), 32.

5. Ibid., 39.

6. In both the 1977 and 1982 studies these figures can be found on p. 43.

7. Quoted in Burton H. Hendrick, *The Life of Andrew Carnegie* (New York: Doubleday Doran, 1932), vol. 2, 50.

8. For an exact description of all penalties see 1986-87 *Manual of the NCAA*, (Shawnee Mission, Kans.: NCAA, 1986), 222-25.

9. Unlike the professional football or basketball leagues, which require the team that signs the free agent to give compensation (draft choices or money) to his former team, the baseball player can, if he chooses, "easily" change employers. In the late 1970s this was particularly true, but in the mid-1980s the free agent market is considerably less aggressive.

10. The reason for this inability is most often the lack of a 2.00 grade point average (on a 4.00 scale) in high school.

11. 1986-87 *NCAA Manual*, 217.

12. Ibid., 223.

13. Ibid., 60-61.

Chapter 6

The NCAA and the Future of Intercollegiate Athletics

THE BUSINESS OF COLLEGE FOOTBALL

Since it is clear that coaches and athletic administrators have used the National Collegiate Athletic Association (NCAA) to organize a cartel and maximize their gain, it is fair to ask how this has affected the schools and the players.

Even persons with only superficial knowledge of sports are aware that college football (and basketball) represents big money. A winning team not only provides publicity for a school, but also translates into millions of dollars in income. The winning teams appear on television and, in the case of basketball, in the NCAA's national tournament. The immense sums these teams earn, along with donations, support a school's athletic program. A university generally feels compelled to field successful teams in these sports because it needs the money to fund other sports that cannot cover their costs with gate receipts, to pay the coaches' salaries, and to maintain or improve the quality of its athletic facilities. Being a football winner is still important for many of the same reasons it was when college sports began, but a winner now helps determine the overall quality of a school's athletic program. The losers, however, in this arrangement — scholastically as well as financially — are often the generators of the income, the athletes themselves.

In the early days of football, coaches were often students and the players were simply the best athletes among them. But as the benefits grew, paid professionals replaced student coaches, and the athletes were widely recruited and often paid. In the NCAA, football coaches from many schools discovered a shared experience. Those trying to develop big-time football teams were up against other coaches trying to do the same thing. The most competitive phase of college athletics was no longer on the field; it was in recruiting student-athletes.

To most, but especially those coaches, the value, in dollars and cents (and larger coaching salaries and better facilities) of a highly skilled blue-chip athlete remains clear. We should not be surprised to find, therefore, that the likelier an athlete is to contribute to a winning team, the greater the resources a school will spend luring him to campus. But while Americans generally expect to pay for a valued service or product, industrywide rules prevent this in college athletics.

The NCAA has always tried to prohibit schools from paying athletes for their services by invoking its own definition of amateurism and by adopting new rules. However, highly skilled athletes continually test these rules because of their enormous value. Meanwhile, the institutions recruiting these athletes face a perplexing dilemma: The NCAA rules tell the athletic department that it can offer only certain things, but common sense tells a recruiter or coach that the athlete is worth much to the team (in victories) and to the program (financially) than the meager compensation the NCAA allows. The pressure to break NCAA rules is, therefore, tremendous, and it is often compounded by fawning alumni who like to help with the recruiting. One logical outcome of this conflict is that universities often provide valuable athletes with compensation far in excess of NCAA regulations. In short, otherwise reputable universities become athletic cheaters.

The inevitable violations of NCAA rules are consequences of policies that disregard or discount the value of skilled athletes. That more rampant cheating does not occur is a tribute, perhaps, to the inherent honesty of most people directly involved in college sports. To put the cheating that does occur in perspective, one can point out that the NCAA has been trying for 80 years to enforce amateurism, yet frequent reports of violations, which hint at the depth of noncompliance throughout the Association, have continued. Thus, cheating on amateur rules is not a new phenomenon.

In its first 25 years, the NCAA produced the Eligibility Code and the Code on Recruiting and Subsidizing Athletes as a method of prohibiting athletic compensation. But the Carnegie Foundation Report, among other investigations, showed how ineffective these codes were. In the late 1940s, the NCAA adopted a Sanity Code, which was repealed by the members shortly after the first schools were unsuccessfully prosecuted under it. Today, an active Enforcement and Compliance Department within the NCAA receives additional help from a private investigative firm, but play-for-pay scandals abound. All of this suggests that the NCAA has failed to keep schools from offering athletes compensation, a failure reflecting its inability to acknowledge that, like King Canute, it can no more prevent coaches from coveting the tremendous value of superior athletes than it can pass a law governing the tides.

NCAA rules that attempt to prohibit athletic compensation have produced other effects the Association could not possibly have anticipated. All other students can sell their skills, or work part-time, but not athletes. The long hours of practice give them little time to earn the expense money the NCAA forbids them. Some students (for example, those with special skills in computer science or business) have begun lucrative businesses while in school and have learned valuable entrepreneurial skills in the process. NCAA athletes, however, cannot engage in the same kind of activities and are specifically forbidden to capitalize on the skills millions of people willingly pay to see.

Most college graduates begin a slow, rather steady climb up the salary ladder. But for 100 or so college athletes each year, it's an instant jump: They sign professional contracts for more money than the average wage earner sees in a lifetime. These financially naive athletes often become victims of unscrupulous agents, managers, and friends. NCAA policies leave them no more prepared to deal with this newfound wealth than the impoverished winner of a state lottery. Some, no doubt, squander their sudden wealth on shiny cars, fast times, and drugs.

While they are on campus, student-athletes often learn more about educational shortcuts than about personal finance. Valuable athletes pass courses even when they skip classes, and they have been known to receive credit for courses in which they never enrolled. It is not at all unusual for a coach or athletic administrator to take special steps to ensure that particular athletes remain eligible. Faced with the loss of a star athlete (and the victories and money he helps generate) coaches and athletic administrators have been known to cajole, harass, and pressure faculty members into accommodating athletes. After all, whose value to the university can more readily be seen on a Saturday afternoon—a star quarterback or an untenured junior professor?

Athletes also find that they can use their special status to avoid legal trouble. If an athlete gets drunk, drives recklessly, or even commits rape, his school or his coach frequently "takes care of it." While a nonathlete might go to jail, probation, community service, or even dropped charges keep a key athlete on the field.

The net effect of the NCAA's often hypocritical pursuit of amateurism has, therefore, been a perversion of the entire educational process and system. For an athletic grant-in-aid, a student gets the privilege of working long hours with no chance to earn the money he needs to participate in normal college activities. Student-athletes do get special privileges, but these privileges often help an athlete escape responsibility, instead of learning skills and values that will be useful off the playing field. Oddly, this perversion stems from the fact that superior players are so valuable to an athletic program that many within the education system itself look the other way to ensure that these athletes continue to participate.

REDUCING THE PROBLEMS

There are several ways to attack the problems caused by the combination of revenue-producing athletics and education. One obvious solution would be to abolish commercial football at all universities. If we hypothesize an agreement to do so among all university presidents, such a cold-turkey solution would indeed eliminate many of the problems mentioned here by simply excluding semiprofessional athletes from campuses.

The history of intercollegiate sports shows, however, that this solution would be short lived. With the loss of big-time football, fans would turn to the next level of collegiate competition to satisfy their appetite for the game. Fraternities, for example, might start an interuniversity league. They would quickly find enough outside interest to play in stadiums and charge admission. Driven by the public recognition and potential television appearances, these teams would begin recruiting actively, and suddenly the cycle would start again. Thus, while it may be interesting to imagine what education would be like without big-time athletics, practically speaking, it would be difficult to abolish sports.

A second and more reasonable solution is to let universities continue to field athletic teams and engage in whatever level of competition they desire, but to recognize the contribution of the athletes and pay them accordingly. Universities could still stage athletic events, but the student-athletes would be compensated for their services in the same way that the coaches, time-keepers, and game officials are compensated.

This solution is, of course, squarely against the NCAA's policy of amateurism. However, the examination of intercollegiate sports conducted in this book suggests no rational explanation for keeping student-athletes in NCAA-enforced servitude. No matter how it is rationalized, the NCAA's policy of amateurism has the effect of preventing athletes from receiving any sort of fair payment and of allowing athletic departments to use the money these athletes generate to pay coaches and build facilities.

Once, back at the turn of the century, professional athletes may have been so flagrantly unscrupulous and so, well, proletarian that those who played sports for the pure enjoyment of it needed recognition as a separate group or class. But this distinction, if it ever existed, has long since disappeared. What, after all, really separates a professional from a grant-in-aid athlete at a school with a major sports program? Both practice long hours, both receive compensation for their athletic skills, and both participate in multimillion dollar industries. The demarcation line blurs even more when NCAA rules allow a student-athlete to turn pro in one sport but remain an amateur in another. Thus, any difference between a student-athlete in a big-time sports program and a professional athlete lies only in the amount of their compensation, not in any special quality the amateur enjoys and the professional lacks.

Obviously the system of intercollegiate athletics that would result under this policy would be very different from the present one. Many changes would take place, but these would be an improvement over the present system and could lead to reductions in the total cost of administering college athletics.

Under this regime, colleges would have no recruiting restrictions. They could contact a high school athlete as often as they liked (or were allowed) and do whatever they felt was necessary (provide gifts, take him to dinner, bring him to campus) to induce him to attend—a situation similar to an employer attempting to hire a new employee. Universities would be restricted during the recruiting period only by their budgets, their imagination, and the law.

When the athlete made his decision, he and the school would sign an agreement similar to the national letter of intent. The contents of this agreement, however, would be negotiated between the school and the athlete, not dictated entirely by the university, as is currently the case. Whereas current NCAA rules allow a school to offer only room, board, and tuition, the athlete would be free to negotiate the best deal for himself, much as anyone else is free to do.

In this new system, high school athletes would face many of the same decisions they currently face when choosing a school. The athlete would still have to decide which school is right for him, only he would have more control over deciding what he was to receive for his talents. In the course of making this decision, the athlete will obtain experience he could readily apply later. Interviewing, negotiating, handling responsibility, and even determining when to delegate it (as in when and who to call in for advice) would be skills the high school athlete would have to develop. Ironically, successful college athletes face exactly the same issues at the end of their college careers when the professional leagues come calling. Under this proposal, a similar process for high school athletes would occur four years earlier.

In this new regime, universities would face an unfamiliar challenge. Each school would have to develop a strategy to maximize the effectiveness of its athletic budget. Should it make large offers to a few high school hotshots, or moderate offers to several above-average athletes, or a combination of both? How many sports teams should it field? How many athletes should it hire and what should these athletes be paid? Universities would not relish a new system entailing so many more decisions, but the recruiting would be no more competitive than it is now, and the overall cost of administering college sports would probably diminish.

Recruiting would become a more straightforward process under this proposal. As matters stand now, schools tend to pursue high school athletes longer than they might if they could simply bid in a talent auction. Because it costs schools little to express interest in high school athletes under the current system, the good athletes attract many schools (sometimes over 100); the recruiting drags on as the schools fight to be one of the 6 that can offer the athlete a paid trip to its campus; and then these 6 schools compete more fiercely to sign the athlete.

Under the new arrangement, a school would know almost immediately if it could afford to compete for an athlete by comparing the offers made by other schools. A school could expedite the decision-making process by leading with its best and final offer. If the athlete accepted or rejected the offer, the school's recruiting involvement would end. Consequently, a school could devote more time to the athletes it could truly afford.

It is also not clear that paying athletes would produce higher athletic costs. Because of the revenue-generating capabilities of basketball and football, these players would attract the most recruiting attention, but universities do not need to pay these athletes anywhere near as much as the professional teams pay them. The training an athlete receives in college, the exposure he receives, and the value of a possible college degree should rightly be included when a salary is negotiated. Thus, a nonstarter in football and basketball might expect a scholarship plus between $100 and $200 a month; a contributor but not a key player might receive between $300 and $600 a month; and a key player might get up to $1,000 a month.

(The method of payment presents another menu of choices to the universities. Schools might make monthly payments, use incentive clauses, or even put the money in a trust fund, payable only when the athlete graduates and passes a drug test.)

With payments like this, schools would quickly find that they could get by with smaller squads. Thus, instead of maintaining a football team with 95 scholarship athletes, schools might field teams with fewer, less specialized athletes. The fact that professional football teams play 18 regular season games with only 50 members indicates that colleges might be able to compete just as effectively during an 11-game season with teams of between 60 and 80 members.

Universities would also have to determine what strategy they wanted to follow for the minor, nonrevenue sports. They might continue to field the same number of teams as they previously did, but since the football and basketball surpluses would go to pay the athletes in those sports, universities would either have to cut back on these sports or find new sources of revenue (alumni donations or university subsidy) to support these sports.

Just as the NCAA now maintains different membership divisions based on a school's athletic ambitions, so would schools be similarly divided under a play-for-pay system. Schools prepared to maintain big-time athletic programs would continue to occupy the top division and receive the lion's share of the public attention. Less ambitious schools with more moderate budgets would be next, and finally, much like Division III now, schools that choose not to pay athletes would comprise a separate division.

What would change is the NCAA's role in intercollegiate sports. Without recruiting and compensation limits, the NCAA would not need complex rules and would not need to monitor the entire country for violations. A tremendous savings would result because the Association would no longer need to meet annually to devise rules to prevent the cheating they were sure they had stopped the previous year. Accordingly, the Compliance and Enforcement Department would disappear.

Under a play-for-pay system, the NCAA could return to its original goals of writing rules and organizing tournaments. One new responsibility it could assume, however, would be to accumulate information about salaries and working conditions at the various universities throughout the country. Much like a consumers' group that reports on the performance of dishwashers, the NCAA could provide information of interest to athletes. Instead of regulating and controlling the market, as they now do, the NCAA would simply help athletes make informed decisions.

Finally comes the question of fairness. Intercollegiate sports has become a large business, and many earn a comfortable living from it. Football and basketball coaches in particular enjoy large salaries and receive additional compensation from their own television shows, sports camps, and endorsements. At the major schools, a six-figure income for these coaches is the rule rather than the exception. In contrast, athletes currently receive only tuition and room and board for their services. Since tuition is worth what the university says it is worth and since many athletes never graduate anyway, it seems like a dubious payment. A play-for-pay system would not guarantee that all athletes receive compensation in excess of a scholarship. It would, however, allow an athlete to be free from NCAA restrictions so that he could negotiate a more rewarding deal.

A third possible solution to the problems caused by the combination of big-time athletics with education, which is related to the play-for-pay idea just discussed, calls for separating sports from college altogether. Instead of being banned, sports teams could exist as individual professional units with which schools could choose to be only nominally affiliated.

No one has ever convincingly explained why athletes have to attend college to pursue a professional sports career. Lawyers and doctors receive specialized training in college but barbers, for example, receive their training in other schools. Why should we force, or try to force, athletes to attend college classes? Surely the training they need to obtain a lucrative professional contract can be provided in a more direct way.

Another professional sports league could be established with teams in each major college town: the Columbus Buckeyes, the Ann Arbor Wolverines, the Lincoln Cornhuskers, and so forth. Schools could affiliate with the nearby team and enjoy the benefits of sponsoring a team without any of the traditional and currently growing problems. Athletes, in turn, could go on with their training for professional careers without pretending to be college students, or they could enroll in classes when their time permitted.

THE NCAA AND THE CFA

Due primarily to the efforts of the CFA, particularly the Universities of Georgia and Oklahoma, the NCAA no longer oversees the televising of college football. The 1984 Supreme Court decision, which ended the NCAA's ability to draw up a football contract between the members and a network, cost the NCAA administration about $5 million dollars in annual revenue. (This money came from the fee the NCAA imposed on all payments for television appearances.) But the Association is far from financially strapped. Its most lucrative event, the Division I Men's National Basketball Tournament, remains popular and highly profitable. Furthermore, the sale of television rights to other, heretofore less well known, NCAA championship events in such sports as gymnastics, swimming, volleyball, and baseball has provided new revenue sources.

Throwing college football television onto the free market naturally produced some winners and some losers. The schools that play exciting football are becoming television favorites, but their payments are not so large as they were under the old NCAA-organized television contract. In that sense, the 1984 decision killed the golden goose.

More games are being shown at the regional level, sometimes in competition with the once sacrosanct national broadcasts. In this way schools that seldom appeared on the NCAA's package are getting more television coverage. In conferences with several popular football schools (the Big 8 and the Pac 10, for example) opponents frequently find themselves enjoying the benefits of having their games against these teams televised.

The losers in this new television alignment seem to be the schools in membership categories other than Division I-A. Under the old agreement, the NCAA required the networks to show several games from each of the other divisions as part of the broadcast package they purchased. Now, however, these schools rarely appear and then generally on public television or minor networks. Thus, one can expect to see more college football but increasingly focused on only the 100 or so well-known schools.

The CFA presents the NCAA with yet another challenge. No doubt the NCAA directors feel some animosity toward the CFA after its court victory, and a natural reaction would be for them to keep a much closer watch on the CFA member schools. This natural tendency may translate into more NCAA investigations and penalties—like the one now facing the University of Georgia. Someone once joked that the initials NCAA stood for Never Compromise Anywhere Anytime. If this joke portrays the truth, the NCAA has ample tools to return the CFA's favor, as long as the CFA members still belong to the NCAA.

The CFA could, of course, leave the NCAA altogether to form a rival athletic association, but this seems unlikely. The NCAA dominates college athletics primarily because it succeeded in its early days so efficiently that competing associations willingly joined the NCAA rather than going it alone. Once the NCAA became the dominant force in college athletics, it began to operate like any other cartel, restricting its product's availability, limiting payments to athletes, and reducing

competition for its products. The NCAA's battle with the Amateur
Athletic Union (AAU) for control over amateur athletics required
presidental intervention in the 1960s, and its battle with the Association of Intercollegiate Athletics for Women (AIAW) resulted in a law
suit and the subsequent demise of the group in 1982. Even the National
Invitational Tournament (NIT), once the most prestigious postseason
collegiate basketball tournament in the country, lost most of its luster
primarily because of the growth of the NCAA's tournament and the
NCAA rules that keep a member from competing in more than one
postseason basketball tournament a year. Whether the NCAA simply
offered a better product in each case or intentionally set out to
eliminate the competition, its current cartel status keeps an effective
check on would-be competitors.

How, then, would the CFA fare if it formed a rival association? Inter-
CFA football competition would present few problems because
relatively few games are played (11, versus a minimum of 25 and often
as many as 40 in a basketball schedule) and most CFA members play
their games with other CFA members. In basketball, however, the
CFA members would find that travel constraints make it impossible to
schedule only fellow CFA members. They would have to schedule at
least some local NCAA teams, and the NCAA might prevent its
members from competing with the CFA. Unless the CFA could bring
enough new members into its association to make regional competition
economical, an important factor in the smaller sports, it could compete
with the NCAA in only one sport—football.

Ultimately, the whole issue of the NCAA's keeping members from
competing with non-NCAA schools might end up in a lengthy and expensive court battle. But if a new association (for example, the CFA)
were to offer features that differed only slightly from the NCAA's, it
seems unlikely that many schools would want to join that new association and then deal with the many attendant obstacles the NCAA might
erect.

Finally, there is the question of how long the CFA can survive.
Unlike the NCAA, which encompasses all sports, CFA members are
bound primarily by their common football interests. As long as the
CFA television ratings and revenue remain high, the CFA can with-
stand possible problems. Indeed, the national exposure necessary
for football programs seeking nationwide recognition can only be obtained through the CFA's television pact, and, thus, the CFA has an
important role in college football. But if CFA football becomes
overexposed, subsets of the group might be tempted to go it on their
own.

THE NCAA 80 YEARS LATER

In December 1905, the forerunner of the NCAA was organized to address the crisis in college football precipitated by chaotic rules that encouraged violence, injury, and death. Today, 80 years later, the NCAA can proudly point out that it has made football considerably safer. In many other areas, however, the NCAA has caused problems rather than prevented them.

Its preoccupation with the appearance of amateurism has allowed the rising tide of intercollegiate sports to improve all fortunes but those of the athletes. Student-athletes practice continually, play the games that fans pay to see, and frequently fail to graduate. Only a small percentage of them ever make handsome salaries as professional athletes. Meanwhile, the coaches, the athletic administrators, the television and radio networks, and even the local vendors who sell State U. paraphernalia, benefit from their work. If amateurism is such a good policy, why is it good only for the athletes? Why is coaching such a highly articulated and lucrative line of work? And why are NCAA executives paid so well?

The mechanism the NCAA set up to catch rule violators has become a source of constant problems. Many questions surround the probity of the NCAA's investigations and the rights of universities and their students, questions that lead the Association into lengthy court conflicts that may not be settled until well after the athlete in question has left school. As we have seen, the NCAA simply cannot monitor all of intercollegiate athletics. Its highly publicized efforts to do so merely indicate that the enforcement mechanism has never worked and that most cheaters escape.

The NCAA's television policy is another area that raised more problems than it settled. Free from NCAA control, schools might have continued to televise their college football contests. No one can say what would have resulted without NCAA intervention, but Americans would certainly have seen more games. Perhaps the clamor for television time would have stimulated the earlier development of such alternative modes of telecasting as cable. Perhaps the NCAA's restrictive policy altered forever the nation's football elite. As we saw, the University of Pennsylvania was among the first schools to realize the benefits from televising games. Without NCAA interference, Penn might have used its telecasting revenue to build a nationally dominant athletic program like that of the more remote and rustic Penn State 200 miles to the west. In the late 1940s, it was not the Georgias and Nebraskas that stood atop the intercollegiate sports world; it was the schools from the East. If one can say that NCAA television helped build these other programs, the reverse must be true of schools like the University of Pennsylvania.

With the NCAA's 1984 conviction on antitrust charges came a delicious sort of irony. When rationalizing its control of intercollegiate sports, the NCAA had always cloaked itself in altruism and, not infrequently, patriotism. Yet it stood convicted of using the same tactics generally associated with the robber barons of the twentieth century. Moreover, President Theodore Roosevelt, who encouraged the formation of the NCAA, rode into office on a reputation for busting the trusts that dominated and manipulated markets in much the same way the NCAA controlled televising college football.

In fact, because so much of what it now does flirts with illegality, the NCAA has acquired its own legal department. It may be difficult to gauge whether the NCAA needs this legal advice because intercollegiate sports has become so complex (for example, the NCAA may want to ensure that the contracts associated with its various tournaments are written so that they are protected from negligence suits) or if the NCAA's efforts to control college athletics forces athletes to seek redress through the courts. Nonetheless, the addition of this legal department testifies to the complex goals of the present Association, which stands in stark contrast to an association begun with a simple idea of writing a safe set of football rules.

Current NCAA activities have carried it into other areas its founders probably did not envision. It maintains an active Governmental Affairs and Joint Legislative Committee to protect its interests in the legislative arena, to shield the Association from any governmental action that might limit its power, and to help it convince the Congress that all it really wants is to foster pure and healthy competition. In short, the NCAA has appointed a committee to lobby the government, just like any other for-profit industry.

A look back over the NCAA's first 80 years makes it clear that the Association's most pronounced successes have been in the fields it was best suited to handle. As an association of coaches and athletic directors, it is well equipped to establish rules and conduct championship tournaments, but not to organize television contracts and police the behavior of thousands of participants in intercollegiate athletics. It comes as no surprise, therefore, that the NCAA's tournaments and rules provide national standards of excellence. The NCAA's regulation of the remaining aspects of intercollegiate sports, however, is an entirely different story and the source of criticism and legal prosecution.

As the Association heads toward the twenty-first century and its one hundredth anniversary, it must address two fundamental problems in intercollegiate sports. The first is the inherent contradiction of amateurism as the NCAA currently defines and treats it. Paying athletes for their performances would go a long way toward solving these problems.

The second problem concerns the size and scope of the athletic programs the NCAA presides over. More and more, college athletic programs break down into one of two types. A small group of about 100 schools maintain multimillion dollar programs that seek national prominence and closely resemble professional sports enterprises. The remaining NCAA members have more moderate goals with much smaller athletic budgets and aspirations. If the NCAA is to direct all intercollegiate sports for the next 80 years, it must relinquish some of its preoccupation with the first group, enact policies that ratify the already obvious differences in the two groups, and assume its original role as arbiter and counselor.

APPENDIX A

The NCAA's First Eligibility Code

The following rules ... are suggested as a minimum:

1. No student shall represent a college or university in any intercollegiate game or contest, who is not taking a full schedule of work as prescribed in the catalogue of the institution.

2. No student shall represent a college or university ... who has at any time received, either directly or indirectly, money, or any other consideration, to play on any team, or ... who has competed for a money prize or portion of gate money in any contest, or who has competed for any prize against a professional.

3. No student shall represent a college or university ... who is paid or received, directly or indirectly, any money, or financial concession, or emolument as past or present compensation for, or as prior consideration or inducement to play in, or enter any athletic contest, whether the said remuneration be received from, or paid by, or at the instance of any organization, committee or faculty of such college or university, or any individual whatever.

4. No student shall represent a college or university ... who has participated in intercollegiate games or contests during four previous years.

5. No student who has been registered as a member of any other college or university shall participate in any intercollegiate game or contest until he shall have been a student of the institution which he represents at least one college year.

6. Candidates for positions on athletic teams shall be required to fill out cards, which shall be placed on file, giving a full statement of their previous athletic records.

Article VII, "Eligibility Rules," NCAA Constitution, 1906.

155

APPENDIX B

The NCAA Code on Recruiting and Subsidizing of Athletes

It is unjustifiable --

(1) For a student to receive any subsidy of monetary value, either directly or indirectly, primarily for his athletic services.

(2) To employ prospective athletes before they matriculate in an institution, or make advance payment to a prospective student for future services, or to make any guarantee of payment which is not conditioned upon the service being performed in advance of the payment, or to make any payment for services at a rate greater than the current rate for other students in the institution.

(3) To permit a boy to participate in intercollegiate contests who has ever received a loan, scholarship aid, remission of fees, or employment, primarily because he is an athlete, through channels not open to non-athletes equally with athletes.

(4) For members of athletic or physical education staffs to recruit athletes by initiating correspondence or conversation, or by arranging for interviews with boys who are prospective athletes.

(5) To promise prospective athletes employment, loans, scholarships, or remission of fees, except as they may be secured by other students through the regular channels of the institution, and those channels should be outside the athletic or physical education departments.

Proceedings of the National Collegiate Athletic Association, 1935, A-II.

(6) For alumni groups, clubs, fraternities, or other organizations to make promises or direct or indirect subsidies to prospective students, primarily for their athletic ability.

(7) To endeavor to persuade a prospective athlete, by offer of a scholarship or job, or by any other means, to transfer from a college where he has made application for admission and has been accepted.

APPENDIX C

Section Four from Principles for the Conduct of Intercollegiate Athletics

Section 4. Principles Governing Financial Aids to Athletes.

Financial aids in the form of scholarships, fellowships or otherwise, even though originating from sources other than persons on whom the recipient may be naturally or legally dependent for support, shall be permitted without loss of eligibility

(a) if approved and awarded on the basis of need by the regular agency established ... for granting of aid to all students, provided [that aid] shall not exceed the amount of tuition for instruction and for stated incidental institution fees, or

(b) if approved and awarded on the basis of qualifications in which high scholarship on the part of the recipient is the major factor and ... provided, however, that the existence of such scholarship, fellowship or other aid and its terms are announced in an official publication of such institution, or

(c) if awarded on the basis of qualifications of which athletic ability is not one ....

In all cases the agency making the award of aid shall give the recipient a written statement of the amount, duration, conditions and terms thereof.

The acceptance of financial aid not permitted by the provisions of this section shall render the recipient ineligible for intercollegiate athletic competition.

Proceedings of the National Collegiate Athletic Association, 1948, 212-13.

(d) Any scholarship or other aid to an athlete shall be awarded only through a regular agency approved by the institution for the granting of aid to all students.

(e) No athlete shall be deprived of financial aids permitted [in] this section because of failure to participate in intercollegiate athletics.

(f) Compensation of an athlete for employment shall be commensurate with the service rendered.

(g) No one shall be denied student aid because he is an athlete.

APPENDIX D

Original Members of the College Football Association (CFA)

The original members of the CFA, as reported in the *Chronicle of Higher Education* (September 2, 1981, p. 6.) were:

University of Alabama
University of Arkansas, Fayetteville
Auburn University
Baylor University
Brigham Young University
Boston College
Clemson University
University of Colorado
Colorado State University
Duke University
University of Florida
Florida State University
University of Georgia
Georgia Institute of Tech.
University of Hawaii
University of Houston
Iowa State University

University of Kansas
Kansas State University
University of Kentucky
Louisiana State University
University of Maryland, College Park
Memphis State University
University of Miami (Florida)
University of Mississippi
Mississippi State University
University of Missouri, Columbia
University of Nebraska, Lincoln
University of New Mexico
University of North Carolina, Chapel Hill
North Carolina State University
North Texas State University
University of Notre Dame

University of Oklahoma
Oklahoma State University
Pennsylvania State University
University of Pittsburgh
Rice University
Rutgers University
San Diego State University
University of South Carolina
Southern Methodist University
University of Southern Mississippi
Syracuse University
University of Tennessee, Knoxville
University of Texas, Austin
University of Texas, El Paso
Texas A & M University

Texas Christian University
Texas Tech University
Tulane University
U.S. Air Force Academy
U.S Military Academy
U.S. Naval Academy
University of Utah
Vanderbilt University
University of Virginia
Virginia Polytechnic Institute
Wake Forest University
West Virginia University
University of Wyoming

Bibliography

BOOKS

Alchian, Armen, and Allen, William. *Exchange and Production: Competition, Coordination, and Control.* 2nd ed. Belmont, Calif.: Wadsworth, 1969.

Bennett, Bruce L., and Van Dalen, Deobold B. *A World History of Physical Education.* Englewood Cliffs, N.J.: Prentice Hall, 1971.

Danzig, Allison. *The History of American Football.* Englewood Cliffs, N.J.: Prentice Hall, 1956.

Demmert, Henry G. *The Economics of Professional Team Sports.* Lexington, Mass.: Lexington Press, 1973.

Dixon, John. *Landmarks in the History of Physical Education.* London: Routledge and Kegan Paul, 1957.

Frey, James. *The Governance of Intercollegiate Athletics.* West Point, N.Y.: Leisure Press, 1982.

Hackensmith, C.W. *History of Education.* New York: Harper and Row, 1966.

Landany, Shaul P., and Machols, Robert E., eds. *Management Science and Sports.* Amsterdam: North-Holland, 1976.

Lowell, Cym H., and Weistart, John C. *The Law of Sports.* New York: Bobbs-Merrill, 1979.

Noll, Roger G., ed. *Government and the Sports Business.* Washington, D.C.: Brookings Institution, 1974.

Olson, Mancur. *The Logic of Collective Action.* Cambridge, Mass.: Harvard University Press, 1965.

Rogers, Frederick R. *The Future of Intercollegiate Athletics.* New York: Columbia University Press, 1929.

Rooney, John F., Jr. *The Recruiting Game: Toward a New System of Intercollegiate Sports.* Lincoln, Neb.: University of Nebraska Press, 1980.

Savage, Howard. *American College Athletics.* Boston: Merrymount Press, 1929.

Shea, Edward J., and Wieman, Elton E. *Administrative Policies for Intercollegiate Athletics.* Springfield, Ill.: Charles B. Thomas, 1967.
Stocking, George W., and Watkins, Myron W. *Cartels in Action.* New York: Twentieth Century Fund, 1940.
Weyand, Alexander M. *The Saga of American Football.* New York: Macmillan, 1955.

DISSERTATIONS

Flath, Arnold W. "The History of Relations between the National Collegiate Athletic Association and the Amateur Athletic Union of the United States." Ph.D. diss., University of Michigan, 1963.
Stagg, Paul. "The Development of the National Collegiate Athletic Association in Relation to Intercollegiate Athletics in the United States." Ph.D. diss., New York University, 1946.

NCAA PUBLICATIONS

All NCAA documents are published by the NCAA, Shawnee Mission, Kansas. The sources most frequently used in this study were:

Annual Report of the NCAA

Manual of the NCAA

Proceedings of the NCAA

Report of the Television Committee

Revenue and Expense of Intercollegiate Athletic Programs, 1977 and 1982, Mitchell Raiborn.

PERIODICALS

New York Times, Sports Illustrated, and *Chronicle of Higher Education* were important sources for information about the activities of the association from 1905 to 1985.

Anderson, Mark. "The Sherman Act and Professional Sports Association Use of Eligibility." *Nebraska Law Review* 47 (January 1968).
Davenport, David S. "Collusive Competition in Major League Baseball." *American Economist* 13 (Fall 1969).
Faith, Roger; McCormick, Robert E.; and Tollison, Robert. "Economics and Metrology: Give 'Em an Inch and They'll Take a Kilometer." Manuscript, Virginia Polytechnic Institute and State University, 1979.
Hochenberg, Phillip R. "The Four Horsemen Ride Again: Cable Communications and College Athletics." *Journal of College and University Law* 5 (Fall 1978).

Hodirii, Mohamed El, and Quirk, James. "An Economic Model of Professional Sports League." *Journal of Political Economy* 79 (Nov./Dec. 1971)

Horn, Stephen. "Intercollegiate Athletics: Waning Amateurism and Rising Professionalism." *Journal of College and University Law* 5 (Fall 1978).

Jones, J. C. H. "The Economics of the National Hockey League." *Canadian Journal of Economics* 2 (Feb. 1969).

Kaplan, William. "An Overview of Legal Principles and Issues Affecting Postsecondary Athletics." *Journal of College and University Law* 5 (Fall 1978).

Keith, Maxwell. "Development in the Application of Antitrust Laws to Professional Team Sports." *Hasting Law Journal* 10 (Nov. 1958).

Koch, James V. "The Economics of 'Big-Time' Intercollegiate Athletics." *Social Science Quarterly* 52 (Sept. 1971).

_____. "A Troubled Cartel: The NCAA." *Law and Contemporary Problems* 38 (Spring 1973).

Martin, Gordon A., Jr. "The NCAA and the 14th Amendment." *New England Law Review* 11 (1976).

Neale, Walter. "The Peculiar Economics of Professional Sports." *Quarterly Journal of Economics* 78 (Feb. 1964).

Pierce, Samuel R., Jr. "Organized Professional Team Sports and Antitrust Law." *Cornell Law Quarterly* 43 (Summer 1958).

Topkis, Jay H. "Monopoly in Professional Sports." *Yale Law Review* 58 (April 1949).

Index

About the Author

PAUL R. LAWRENCE is an economist with Price Waterhouse in Washington, D.C. He has worked for Arthur D. Little, Inc., and Chase Econometrics, and his area of expertise includes applied microeconomics and industrial organization. He is also an avid football fan and a high school and college football official. Dr. Lawrence holds a B.A. from the University of Massachusetts, Amherst, and an M.A. and a Ph.D. from Virginia Polytechnic Institute and State University.